Healers and Researchers

Healers and Researchers

Physicians, Biologists, Social Scientists

Judy McClure

RAINTREE
STECK-VAUGHN
PUBLISHERS

A Harcourt Company

Austin • New York
www.steck-vaughn.com

Published by Raintree Steck-Vaughn Publishers, an imprint of Steck-Vaughn Company

CREATED IN ASSOCIATION WITH MEDIA PROJECTS INCORPORATED
C. Carter Smith, *Executive Editor*
Carter Smith III, *Managing Editor*
Judy McClure, *Principal Writer*
Ana Deboo, *Project Editor*
Bernard Schleifer, *Art Director*
John Kern, *Cover Design*
Karen Covington, *Production Editor*

RAINTREE STECK-VAUGHN PUBLISHERS STAFF
Walter Kossmann, *Publishing Director*
Kathy DeVico, *Editor*
Richard Dooley, *Design Project Manager*

Photos on front cover, clockwise from top left:
Biruté Galdikas, Gerty Cori, Mae Jemison, Rachel Carson

Photos on title page, top to bottom: Anna Freud, Jane Cooke Wright, Margaret Mead, Sara Josephine Baker

Acknowledgments listed on page 80 constitute part of this copyright page.

Library of Congress Cataloging-in-Publication Data
McClure, Judy.
    Healers and researchers: physicians, biologists, social scientists / Judy McClure.
        p.   cm. — (Remarkable women: past and present)
    Summary: Presents short biographical profiles of women notable for their contributions to medicine, from cardiologist Maude Abbott to physician and educator Marie Zakrzewska.
    ISBN 0-8172-5734-9
    1. Women physicians—Biography Juvenile literature. 2. Women scientists—Biography Juvenile literature. [1. Women in medicine. 2. Physicians. 3. Scientists. 4. Women—Biography.] I. Title. II. Series: Remarkable women.
R692.M37   2000
509.2'2—dc21
[B]   99-13010
                                                        CIP

Printed and bound in the United States
1 2 3 4 5 6 7 8 9 0 LB 03 02 01 00 99

C O N T E N T S

INTRODUCTION

THE WORD "SCIENCE" COMES FROM THE LATIN *SCIENTIA*, OR "KNOWLEDGE." And all the women in this book have made important contributions to the life sciences and social sciences. That is, they strove to learn about different kinds of living creatures, about how the body functions and malfunctions, the processes of the human mind, or, on a larger scale, how societies work. They possess in common a curiosity about and delight in the world, the willingness to work on a project for years, and the ability to draw conclusions from even the tiniest, subtlest details.

Scientific research can be a solitary pursuit, requiring long hours (or weeks, or years) alone or in close collaboration with only a few people. Barbara McClintock worked in her lab studying genetics without an assistant, without even a telephone. She found out that she had won the Nobel Prize when she heard it on the radio.

Some scientists actually study other people. The anthropologist Margaret Mead studied the cultures of native peoples living as far away as New Guinea and considered her findings in the light of her own 20th-century American society. Beatrice Webb studied society through its economic practices. The psychoanalyst Anna Freud sought to understand the workings of her patients' minds and to help them solve their problems. The archaeologist Kathleen Kenyon learned about societies from a much greater remove. By digging up and examining artifacts from ancient cultures, she acquired information about cultures that had been extinct for centuries.

The search for data can be almost as adventurous as the exploits of a swashbuckling pirate. Roberta Bondar and Mae Jemison, both physicians, have conducted experiments in outer space. Sylvia Earle has traveled the opposite direction, into another vast unexplored

region, the ocean, to study the creatures there. Ynes Mexia criss-crossed the jungles of South America while collecting plant samples.

Often society has made it difficult for women scientists. In 1906 *American Men of Science*, one of the most useful reference books for biographical information about scientists, was published for the first time. Every few years an updated edition came out with a smattering of women in it, but it wasn't until 1968 that the series was retitled *American Men and Women of Science*. By then the Nobel Prize won by Gerty Cori and her husband, Carl, for their work on metabolism was over two decades in the past.

Women doctors in the 19th century had especially many obstacles to overcome. It was believed that women should not concern themselves with sickness and suffering. Many men were too embarrassed to study the human body in mixed company, and some patients refused to consult a woman physician. Emily and Elizabeth Blackwell, Marie Zakrzewska, Sophia Jex-Blake, and Elizabeth Garrett Anderson all opened medical schools to help other women qualify for the profession.

The desire to pass on the results of their work is another quality that most women in this book have in common. Rachel Carson worked to warn the public about the dangerous effects of pollution on the environment to the public. Virginia Apgar developed a test for evaluating a newborn baby's health that has saved thousands. Anna Williams developed treatments for diseases such as diphtheria and rabies. Maria Merian drew gorgeous, accurate pictures of insects to help document species for other entomologists. Their thirst for knowledge, once satisfied, gave rise to the desire to make use of that knowledge to heal or to teach.

Photos top left Roberta Lynn Bondar, bottom left Joycelyn Elders,
top right Lady Mary Montagu, bottom right Alice Hamilton.

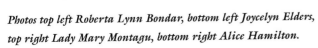

Maude Abbott (1869–1940)

Physician, cardiologist

THE CANADIAN PHYSICIAN MAUDE ABBOTT HAD a long and interesting relationship with McGill University in Montreal. She began there as an undergraduate, receiving her degree in 1884. She wanted to go to McGill's medical school, too, but, as a woman, she wasn't eligible. Instead, she earned an M.D. at Bishop's College in Lenoxville, Quebec, and studied abroad. By 1900 she was back at McGill, and she stayed until her retirement in 1936. Starting as an assistant curator at the university's medical museum, she became head curator, lecturer, and, in 1925, assistant professor. In 1910, nine years before they began accepting women students, McGill awarded Abbott an honorary medical degree.

Abbot became internationally known for her expertise on the heart. She made an analysis of 1,000 congenital heart cases and published a book, *Atlas of Congenital Cardiac Disease* (1936). She was an honorary member of the California Heart Association and the Cardiac Society of Great Britain and Ireland.

Dr. Abbott also helped advance the acceptance of women in medicine. While on leave from McGill, she taught at the Woman's Medical College of Pennsylvania. She was instrumental in helping women gain membership into the Montreal Medico-Chirurgical Society, an important group for surgeons. A prolific writer, she was the editor of the *Canadian Medical Association Journal* and published almost 100 papers during her successful career.

Louisa Aldrich-Blake (1865–1925)

Surgeon, hospital administrator

LOUISA ALDRICH-BLAKE CAME FROM THE LARGE family of Reverend Frederick Aldrich and Louisa Blake Morrison. By the age of 17 she knew she wanted to become a doctor, and five years later she enrolled at the London School of Medicine for Women. During her academic studies, she received many honors and was the first woman awarded a Master in Surgery.

She spent her entire career, from 1895 to 1925, at the Elizabeth Garrett Anderson Hospital. During her time there, she worked her way up to senior surgeon. At the same time, she worked at the Royal Free Hospital in anesthesia and surgery, and established a midwifery unit there. She was appointed Dean at her alma mater, the London School of Medicine, and during her 11 years there, doubled its size.

Dr. Aldrich-Blake's surgical technique was well respected by her peers and patients. With her deliberate style and attention to detail, she had very few cases of patient shock following surgery. She was as thorough with her administrative duties as she was with her medical practices. Although she never considered herself a champion of women's rights—she wanted to be judged on her skills as a doctor—her outstanding work paved the way for future women in medicine.

Hattie Elizabeth Alexander (1901–1968)

Bacteriologist, pediatrician

DR. HATTIE ALEXANDER DISCOVERED A CURE FOR influenzal meningitis, a disease caused by *Hemophilus influenzae* bacteria. Meningitis causes swelling of the membranes surrounding the brain and spinal cord, and this form of meningitis was, at the time, always fatal. Working in the laboratory at Columbia-Presbyterian Medical Center in New York

City, Alexander found that the traditional procedure for creating a serum to counteract bacterial disease wasn't effective with influenzal meningitis. So she collaborated with the immunochemist Michael Heidelberger to figure out a new method. By 1941 they had succeeded in reducing the mortality of the disease by 80 percent, and later by ten percent more.

Alexander was also one of the first people to understand that the DNA of bacteria could change, causing resistance to specific antibiotics. She and a scientist named Grace Leidy devised a technique to alter the DNA of *Hemophilus influenzae* bacteria. Their research supported the theory of the relationship between DNA and inherited traits.

Alexander was a popular teacher. She didn't enjoy lecturing but preferred for students to observe patients firsthand. She won many honors and became the first female president of the American Pediatric Society in 1964. An active person, she loved traveling and riding in her speedboat. Alexander and her companion, Dr. Elizabeth Ufford, lived for many years in Port Washington, New York.

Dorothy Hansine Andersen (1901–1963)
Pathologist

As a student at Johns Hopkins University in Baltimore, Dorothy Andersen worked in Dr. Florence Sabin's laboratory and had two papers published. Still, women doctors were not yet fully accepted, and although Andersen had a brilliant record, she was denied a surgical residency. She decided to devote herself to research rather than medical practice.

In 1935 Andersen began working at Babies Hospital at the Columbia-Presbyterian Medical Center in New York City. Her first interest was in heart defects in infants. During World War II, Andersen taught a course on the anatomy and embryology of the heart that became a requirement for all heart surgeons at Babies Hospital.

Shortly after she arrived at Babies Hospital, Andersen made an important discovery. During an autopsy of a child thought to have died from a nutritional disease, Andersen found an unusual condition. After further research, she identified and named a new disease: cystic fibrosis. People who have cystic fibrosis are born with it, and they have difficulty digesting food and breathing. Patients tend to live longer today, but at the time they died in childhood. Continuing her research, Andersen eventually developed a simple diagnostic tool.

Dr. Andersen was often criticized for her independence, her unfeminine love of outdoor sports, and her disheveled appearance. But she had many supporters who appreciated her eccentricity and praised her dedication to her work. She died of lung cancer when she was 62.

Elizabeth Garrett Anderson (1836–1917)
Physician, women's rights activist

When Elizabeth Garrett Anderson first tried to enter medical school, the other students strongly protested her acceptance, and her admittance was revoked—women simply weren't allowed to become doctors. Anderson persisted, though. She became England's first woman physician and worked diligently so that other women could practice medicine, too. In 1872, with Sophia Jex-Blake, she opened the New Hospital for Women in London. It is now named for her.

Born in London, Elizabeth Garrett resolved to become a doctor after she met Elizabeth Blackwell, the first American woman M.D. Garrett became a surgical nurse at Middlesex Hospital in London, and doctors were so impressed with her work that they began inviting her to see patients with them. Since no university would accept her as a medical student, she got a license from the Society of Apothecaries' Hall. Then she opened a clinic for women and children. As soon as France began allowing women to study medicine in 1868, Garrett went to Paris. She earned her M.D. from the Sorbonne in 1870.

In 1871 she married James Skelton Anderson and started a family, but she continued to be active in medicine and other fields. She was one of the first women to serve on the London School Board, and her enthusiasm for women's rights even rivaled that of her famous suffragist sister, Millicent Garrett Fawcett. At the age of 71, Anderson became mayor of the town of Adelburgh, where her family had settled in 1841. She had a long and productive life as a physician, politician, and supporter of women in medicine.

Valerie Edmée André (1922–)
Army surgeon

BETWEEN 1945 AND 1954, FRANCE FOUGHT THE Indochinese War for control of Vietnam, Laos, and Cambodia. One of the heroes of that war was Dr. Valerie André. For 120 rescue missions, André

flew a helicopter to pick up wounded soldiers, gave immediate treatment, and then transported them to a hospital. This brave work earned her one of France's highest military honors, the *Croix de guerre*, three times. In 1953 she received the Legion of Merit from the United States.

André had always been fearless. She rode a motorcycle at 13 years old and took flying lessons at 16. Her medical studies at Strasbourg University were interrupted in 1943 when the arrival of the Nazis forced her to flee to Paris. Specializing in brain surgery, she completed her degree in 1948 at the University of Paris. She soon joined the French army.

In one of Dr. André's most daring missions, she parachuted into a remote area and spent three weeks treating soldiers for typhus. It took several days of travel by foot through the jungles of Laos to return to her post. Along the way Vietnamese villagers who had heard of her impressive jump brought her to take care of their sick, too.

By 1970 André had achieved the rank of colonel. She went on to become France's first woman general.

Virginia Apgar (1909–1974)
Anesthesiologist, physician

WHEN BABIES ARE BORN, DOCTORS EVALUATE them on five things: pulse, respiration, muscle tone, color, and reflexes. Dr. Virginia Apgar created this system and introduced it in 1952. Now, every day and all around the world, babies are given an "Apgar Score" right after birth. Before the Apgar Score, babies were not evaluated immediately. Serious, but treatable, ailments were missed.

Growing up in New Jersey, Apgar was an excellent student who enjoyed math and science. In 1925 she went to Mount Holyoke College in Massachusetts, where she did well academically, while also—with characteristic energy—doing sports, working for the newspaper, playing violin, and acting in plays.

In 1933 Apgar was one of the first women to graduate from Columbia University's medical school. She specialized in surgery and performed operations for two years before deciding to study anesthesiology. Anesthesiologists work in operating rooms helping to control patients' pain by giving them medication to cause unconsciousness or numbness. Before Apgar focused on anesthesiology, these services were performed by nurses.

Apgar had many successes in medicine. One of her most important achievements was establishing the department of anesthesiology at Columbia-Presbyterian Medical Center. She also excelled as director of research for the March of Dimes, an organization committed to the prevention and treatment of birth defects. A kind woman who loved helping

others, she always carried medical equipment in her purse in case her skills were needed. Apgar was a great doctor, researcher, teacher, and leader. Her effect on maternal and infant health care will be evident for many generations.

Artemisia II, Queen of Caria (4th century B.C.E.)
Botanist, medical researcher

ARTEMISIA RULED CARIA IN ASIA MINOR AFTER her husband, King Mausolus, died around 352 B.C.E. A group of her subjects, the Rhodians, thought their new queen would be an easy target for attack. But Artemisia proved them wrong, defeating them soundly.

Medical wisdom during Artemisia's lifetime held that the body contained four humors: blood, yellow bile, black bile, and phlegm. Obtaining the proper balance of these humors was considered essential to achieving good health. Hoping to learn to control the humors, Artemisia gathered herbs and tested their effects. One of the earliest botanists, she was praised for her wide-ranging familiarity with herbs and their medicinal uses.

Artemisia is remembered in the worlds of medicine and of history. A genus of plants, *Artemisia*, is named after her; it includes wormwood and

sagebrush. She also erected an elaborate tomb, the Mausoleum of Halicarnassus, in honor of her husband, King Mausolus. Now destroyed, it was one of the famed Seven Wonders of the World.

Charlotte Auerbach (1899–1994)
Geneticist

CHARLOTTE AUERBACH CAME FROM A JEWISH family in Germany with a tradition of science. Both her father and grandfather were scientists. She was a student at the Kaiser Wilhelm Institute in Berlin when the Nazi party came into power in the early 1930s, and she was forced to flee Germany. Moving to Scotland, she continued her Ph.D. studies at the Institute of Animal Genetics, where she spent the rest of her career.

At the institute Auerbach met Dr. Herman Müller, who introduced her to the study of genetic mutations. Information about our traits are stored on genes in our cells, and mutations are changes in those genes. Auerbach used fruit flies, or *Drosophila*, and the fungus *Neurospora* in her research. She was the first to discover that exposure to mustard gas and other chemicals caused genetic mutations.

Understanding what sorts of things caused mutations led Auerbach to consider how scientists might make beneficial changes in genes. She was a pioneer in this field, which is known as genetic engineering. She published many papers and books, including *Genetics in the Atomic Age* (1956). She also taught at the University of Edinburgh and was awarded the Darwin Medal in 1976 by the Royal Society.

Florence Merriam Bailey (1863–1948)
Ornithologist, zoologist

FLORENCE MERRIAM HAD ALWAYS ENJOYED NATURE and became interested in ornithology while she was a student at Smith College in Massachusetts. She wrote a few articles about the subject, but it was not until she had the misfortune to contract tuberculosis that she devoted herself to the science more fully. She traveled to the southwest United States to

> "The blue jay comes with a dash and a flourish. As Thoreau says, he 'blows the trumpet of winter.' Unlike the chickadee, whose prevailing tints match the winter sky, and whose gentle *day-day-day* chimes with the softly falling snows, the blue jay would wake the world up. His 'clarionet' peals over the villages asleep in the snow-drifts as if it would rouse even the smoke that drowses over their white roofs. He brings the vigor and color of winter."
>
> FLORENCE MERRIAM BAILEY
> *Birds Through an Opera Glass,* 1893

recover and, while there, wrote three books, including *Birds of Village and Field* (1898).

When she was healthy again, Florence went to live with her brother in Washington, D.C. There she met the naturalist Vernon Bailey, whom she married in 1899. They were a good team and worked together for many years, exploring, observing, and writing about nature. She contributed to several of his books, including *Wild Animals of Glacier National Park* (1918) and *Cave Life of Kentucky* (1933).

Bailey also continued her own career. She helped to found the District of Columbia's Audubon Society. In 1929 she became the first woman elected a fellow of the American Ornithologists' Union. Two years later that organization honored her with the first Brewster Medal ever given to a woman.

Florence Bailey published her final book, *Among the Birds in the Grand Canyon National Park*, in 1939. Her observations about the natural world, especially birds, are still important to those who study and enjoy the environment.

Sara Josephine Baker (1873–1945)
Physician, public health administrator

WE NOW KNOW THAT CONTAGIOUS DISEASES ARE spread by germs, but in the early 1900s many did not understand this fact. Dr. Sara Josephine Baker revolutionized health care by implementing basic hygiene education and preventative medicine. Amazingly, a group of doctors petitioned New York City's mayor, saying that her work "was ruining medical practice by its results in keeping babies well."

Baker decided to become a doctor after her father died from typhoid fever when she was 16 years old. She graduated from the Women's Medical College in New York in 1898 and opened a medical practice with her close friend Dr. Florence M. Laighton. In 1901 she took extra work as an inspector for the New York City Health Department and saw firsthand the appalling living conditions of the city's poor. She became famous for capturing "Typhoid Mary" Mallon, a cook who infected numerous families, but her most sustained work was in improving children's health. In 1908 Baker and a team of 30 nurses began teaching mothers about bathing children, ventilating their apartments, breast-feeding, and proper clothing. That summer 1,200 fewer infants died than during the summer before. Such successes pushed New York City to create the first tax-supported division of child hygiene.

Baker contributed to medicine and social change throughout her life. She invented a new method for administering infection-preventing eyedrops to newborn babies. She established groups known as Little Mothers' Leagues to teach young girls how to help their mothers take care of their infant siblings.

She wrote books and articles, and was active in many organizations, including the Babies' Welfare Association, the New York Association for Improving the Conditions of the Poor, and the College Women's Equal Suffrage League.

Ruth Fulton Benedict (1887–1948)
Anthropologist

Ruth Benedict's early life was somewhat unsettled. Her father died when she was two, and her mother moved the family several times. After graduating from Vassar College in 1909, she spent time in Europe; did social work in Buffalo, New York; taught school in Pasadena and Los Angeles, California; and moved to New York City to marry Stanley Benedict. But in 1919 she began to study with the famous anthropologist Franz Boas at Columbia University. She would work with him for the next two decades and was associated with Columbia for the rest of her life.

Benedict began by studying Native American tribes, including the Zuni, Kwakiutl, and Blackfoot. Instead of simply documenting their practices, as many others did, she tried to understand activities in the larger context of their culture and, then, to compare it to her own society. She felt that psychological characteristics could be applied to whole societies. She wrote about this in *Patterns of Culture* (1934), a book that is still considered very important, even among anthropologists who disagree with her concepts. Among her other books are *Race: Science and Politics* (1940), a discussion of and argument against racism, and *The Chrysanthemum and the Sword* (1946), a study of Japanese society.

Margaret Mead was one of Benedict's star students at Columbia, and the two had a long-term relationship. Benedict was an active member of several anthropological associations. She was also the editor of the *Journal of American Folklore* and served as head of both the American Ethnological Society and the American Anthropological Association.

Elizabeth Blackwell (1821–1910)
Emily Blackwell (1826–1910)
Physicians

Samuel and Hannah Blackwell provided all seven of their children, girls and boys, with the same education. True progressives, they supported women's rights and abolition. In 1832 they moved from England to the United States, hoping to revive their failing sugar business. Sadly, Samuel died of malaria in 1838, leaving the family in debt. When his daughters Elizabeth and Emily decided to become doctors, they both had to teach school for years to save the necessary money.

Several universities rejected Elizabeth before she was accepted by Geneva Medical College in New York in 1847. It wasn't that Geneva supported women's rights, but the faculty there recognized that she was exceptionally qualified. They turned the final decision over to the students, who voted to admit her, mostly as a joke. Two years later Elizabeth graduated at the top of her class, and became the first woman M.D. in the United States. She went to Europe for her clinical work and, while there, contracted an infection that blinded her in one eye and made it impossible for her to pursue a career in surgery, as she had intended.

Elizabeth returned to New York City and opened a dispensary where poor women and children could come to receive medical care. Her sister Emily, who in the meantime had gotten her medical degree from Western Reserve University in Ohio, joined her. Together with another pioneering woman physician, Marie Zakrzewska, the sisters turned the dispensary into the New York Infirmary for Women and Children. Emily took on the primary responsibility for running the infirmary, and it expanded quickly under her talented leadership. In 1859 she and Elizabeth added the Woman's Medical College to their facility. At last they had created a place where women patients could receive expert care from highly trained physicians of their own sex.

After 1869 Elizabeth lived and practiced in England. Emily ran the college until 1899, when she referred all her students to the newly coeducational Cornell University medical school. The Blackwells died within a few weeks of each other in 1910.

Marie Boivin (1773–1841)
Midwife

MARIE BOIVIN WAS BORN IN MONTREUIL, FRANCE. Married at the age of 24, she gave birth to a daughter. After the early death of her husband, she began working at the School of Midwifery at the Hôtel Dieu, a large hospital in Paris. There, she studied with Marie Louise Lachapelle, the head midwife, and received her diploma in 1800.

Marie Boivin made many discoveries about female anatomy. She invented a speculum to aid in examining the cervix and was the first person to listen to a fetus' heart with a stethoscope. One of her textbooks, *Traité des maladies de l'uterus et des annexes* (1833, Treatise on the diseases of the uterus and its related parts), was used for many years in France and Germany. She also translated many texts on gynecology from English.

Boivin did receive some recognition for her skills. King Frederick William III of Prussia awarded her the Order of Merit in 1814. In 1827 the University of Marburg in Germany awarded her an honorary medical degree.

Roberta Lynn Bondar (1945–)
Neurobiologist, astronaut

ROBERTA BONDAR, THE FIRST CANADIAN WOMAN astronaut, spent her childhood making model rockets, playing with chemistry sets, trying to communicate with outer space, and collecting NASA posters and badges. Her college studies at the University of Guelph in Ontario were in agriculture, but she then became interested in pathology and neurobiology. She earned a Ph.D. from the University of Toronto in 1974 and her M.D. from McMaster University in 1977. She was ready to begin the process of becoming an astronaut.

The opportunity for space travel comes after several years of preparation and training. Bondar's preparation began in 1983, when she and five others were chosen to join the Canadian Astronaut Program. For the next eight years, she combined her astronaut training with teaching, researching the medical aspects of space travel, and practicing medicine. In 1990 she was chosen by NASA as a payload specialist for the International Microgravity Laboratory mission. Her eight-day journey took place in January 1992 on the space shuttle *Discovery*.

Dr. Bondar eventually left the Canadian Space Agency but continues her research in neurology and pathology. She is also interested in educating young people about environmental issues and encouraging girls in math and science. She has received many awards, including honorary degrees from over 20 universities. She has an elementary school named for her and is a role model for young people around the world.

Alice Middleton Boring (1883–1955)
Biologist, herpetologist

ALICE BORING STARTED A TRADITIONAL CAREER IN the United States, then spent nearly 30 quite untraditional years in China. She earned her undergraduate and graduate degrees at Bryn Mawr College in Pennsylvania, focusing on biology and genetics. While there, she was a student of the biologist Nettie

Stevens. Boring taught at the University of Maine from 1910 until 1918, when she accepted a job at Peking Union Medical College.

Dr. Boring's new life in China inspired a change in her scientific interests, too. She became increasingly interested in herpetology—studying the amphibians and reptiles of the region. Throughout her career at the college and later at Peking University, she influenced Chinese students, both with her knowledge of herpetology and with her western scientific training. For western scientists, who knew little about China's animal life, she was a valuable resource.

When the Japanese invaded China in 1937, Boring was sent to a concentration camp. A year later she was released to the United States, but she soon returned and developed cautious support for the Chinese Communist party. Although she considered China her home, Boring spent the last five years of her life in America, so she could be near her invalid sister.

Louyse Bourgeois (1563–1636)
Obstetrician, midwife

LOUYSE BOURGEOIS STUDIED MIDWIFERY WITH Ambroise Paré, a famous French obstetrician and surgeon. Her husband, Martin Boursier, was an assistant to Paré. Bourgeois worked with poor women in Paris for five years after she completed her training. She was then qualified to join the guild of midwives.

Queen Marie de Médicis was one of Bourgeois's patients. The midwife was present at seven royal births. By devising new ways to deal with problems that arose during and after childbirth, Bourgeois saved many newborns and mothers. For example, her method for resuscitating unconscious newborns was to transfer warm wine from her own mouth to the baby's mouth to clear the mucous and allow it to breathe.

Bourgeois published a long explanation of her techniques in 1608. The work included information on female anatomy, stages of pregnancy, and preventing miscarriages. She promoted proper nutrition and was the first to treat anemia with iron. The knowledge she passed on was useful to doctors and midwives for the next century.

Puerperal Fever

Louyse Bourgeois was once accused of causing the death of a distinguished patient. The Duchess of Orléans died of puerperal fever, an infection that sets in during delivery and can be avoided if the attending practitioner is careful about hand-washing. Bourgeois defended herself, speaking out against the unsanitary habits of the male physicians who had also attended the duchess. Indeed, the high esteem in which Bourgeois was generally held seems to support her claims. Puerperal fever became more common as fewer midwives attended births and men took over that role.

Sara Elizabeth Branham (1888–1962)
Bacteriologist, physician

MENINGITIS, AN EXTREMELY SERIOUS DISEASE, IS an infection of the membranes surrounding the brain and spinal cord. Mostly, it afflicts children, and sufferers who don't die from it may be left blind, deaf, or mentally impaired. In the early 1900s, it was treated with an injection of antiserum prepared using the infection-causing bacteria. But antiserum for one type of meningitis would not work on the next form that struck.

Sara Branham helped find a new, better way of treating meningitis. Branham earned her Ph.D. in bacteriology from the University of Chicago in 1923 and started work on her M.D. In 1927 she accepted a job at the Hygienic Laboratory of the United States, now the National Institutes of Health. She worked there for the next 30 years, only taking time out to finish her M.D.

In 1928 a new meningitis epidemic swept the world. Branham traveled to Europe to collect meningococci bacteria samples. Comparing these to samples she had collected in the United States, she eventually identified three major strains. By 1937 she was able to report that a family of drugs known as sulfa drugs were effective against all forms of meningitis. During World War II, the disease struck again, but sulfa drugs helped prevent another epidemic.

Elizabeth Gertrude Knight Britton (1858–1934)
Botanist

Elizabeth Britton has one general group of mosses (genus *Bryobrittonia*) named for her and 15 subgroups, or species. Over her career, she published more than 340 scientific papers. Although she didn't have an advanced degree and did much of her work unofficially, she was considered an outstanding professional scientist by her colleagues.

Elizabeth and her husband, Nathaniel, often worked together. They conducted several field trips to the West Indies. Nathaniel was a botany professor

at Columbia University in New York, and Elizabeth took charge of the moss collection there— although not hired to do so. The couple were also founders of the New York Botanical Garden. In 1896 Nathaniel became the first director, and, as usual, Britton participated informally. In 1912 she was named honorary curator of mosses.

As a member of the Woman's National Science Club in the 1890s, Britton urged other women to study mosses. A network of female collectors soon formed, and they contributed samples to her collections. Then, with her friend Annie Smith Morrill, Britton founded the William Sullivant Moss Society, now known as the American Bryological Society. Toward the end of her career, Britton's interest turned to wildflowers. She founded the Wild Flower Preservation Society of America in 1902.

Joyce Brothers (1929–)
Psychologist, media personality

In 1955, hoping to supplement the family income, Dr. Joyce Brothers appeared on the quiz show "The $64,000 Question." In preparation, she had memorized a 20-volume encyclopedia on boxing. She won the $64,000—and went on to defeat

a panel of boxing legends in a challenge show. Her television career continued, and soon she was using her training as a psychologist.

A native New Yorker, Brothers received her Ph.D. from Columbia University in 1953 and taught at Columbia and Hunter College. In 1958 she became an incredible success as the host of her own radio and television programs. The format of the shows, unusual at the time, allowed viewers to call in for advice about relationships, sex, raising children, or other worries.

Some psychologists have felt that Brothers's advice is too simplistic, or that the public forum is inappropriate. But, overall, her work has brought her respect from colleagues and the adoration of her audience. She stresses that she tries to be a bridge between the public and the world of psychology, always advising counseling when necessary. Although she no longer has her own show, she makes guest appearances on television and radio, and has a syndicated newspaper column. Her books have been translated into many languages.

Rachel Fuller Brown (1898–1980)
Biochemist

Funguses can grow almost anywhere. Some kinds cause infections in humans; others ruin fabrics or paper. Farmers know that funguses may harm their plants. Fortunately, many such infections can be treated with nystatin, which was discovered by Rachel Brown and Elizabeth Hazen in the late 1940s.

Brown was raised by her mother after her father abandoned the family when she was 12. She did not think she would be able to go to college, but a wealthy family friend paid her tuition to Mount Holyoke. She earned her Ph.D. in organic chemistry and bacteriology from the University of Chicago. In 1926 she started work at the New York State Department of Health, where she remained for four decades. She and Hazen—a mycologist, or fungus identification specialist—began collaborating in 1948.

Their work involved looking for naturally occurring fungicides, the microorganisms that kill fungus, in soil. They isolated the substance that they eventually named nystatin from a soil sample that Brown collected while on vacation in Virginia. By 1954 nystatin had begun to be used in many ways: to treat the skin infection ringworm, Dutch elm disease in trees, and even to prevent damage to paintings after a flood in Florence, Italy, in 1966.

Brown and Hazen could have earned millions of dollars from nystatin. Instead, they decided all profits should go back into research. Not only did they make an important contribution to the world, they made other scientists' discoveries possible as well.

Mary Whiton Calkins (1863–1930)
Psychologist

MARY CALKINS WAS ONE OF THE FIRST WOMEN psychologists, but she didn't start out in the field. After graduating from Smith College in 1885, she taught Greek at Wellesley College, not far from her family's home in Newton, Massachusetts.

At the time, Wellesley's psychology department was new, and Calkins was soon asked to join. She agreed, and quickly prepared herself, completing Ph.D. courses in philosophy and psychology at Clark and Harvard universities. Although she had her professors' support, she was refused a degree because she was female. Luckily, that formality was unimportant to Wellesley, where Calkins spent her long career.

Calkins set up one of the first psychology laboratories at an American college. There she conducted experiments on such issues as dreams, memory, and color theory. Unlike most psychologists of her time, who tried to study behavior separately from emotions and thoughts, she stressed the importance of an independent, conscious self. Calkins was a well-liked

teacher and friend, who was known for living according to the philosophies she taught. She supported the Consumers' League, the Civil Liberties Union, and was a pacifist. Both the American Psychological Association and the American Philosophical Association chose her as their first woman president.

Rachel Louise Carson (1907–1964)
Biologist, ecologist, writer

RACHEL CARSON'S CHILDHOOD IS A REFLECTION of her career. She loved playing in the Pennsylvania woods, learning about plant and animal life. She also loved writing and had her first piece published when she was ten years old. Writing about the environment became Carson's hallmark. Her first books, *Under the Sea Wind* (1941), *The Sea Around Us* (1951), and *The Edge of the Sea* (1955), focused on the science and ecology of the oceans.

Carson's most famous book was *Silent Spring* (1962). She wrote it after receiving a letter from a friend who asked if DDT could be responsible for the death of many birds on her property. DDT (short for dichlorodiphenyl-trichloroethane) was a pesticide that was sprayed from airplanes over large areas of land to control mosquitoes. Carson had already given some thought to the dangerous effects chemicals might have on the environment; the letter from her friend inspired her to write about it.

She knew her book would be controversial. Agriculture was dependent on pesticides and herbicides for growing crops. People did not understand that their actions affected the health of other living things. After *Silent Spring* was published, pesticide

manufacturers tried to discredit her work. But many private citizens agreed with her research. President John F. Kennedy directed his science advisory committee to study the use of pesticides. They confirmed Carson's research and supported legislation banning DDT. The environmental laws and awareness we have today are possible because of Rachel Carson's work.

Margaret Cavendish, Duchess of Newcastle (1623–1673)
Science writer

THROUGH HER STRONG PERSONALITY, MARGARET Cavendish—often called "Mad Madge" by her contemporaries—was an eccentric presence in the 17th-century scientific world. She was not a groundbreaking scientist and even had some outlandish ideas, but she was an early feminist and left her mark by making scientific study more acceptable for women.

Margaret was born in Essex, England, and became a companion to Queen Henrietta Maria. In 1644, during a civil war, she followed the queen into exile in France. There, she married a nobleman named William Cavendish. His brother, Charles, was a scientist, and he introduced her to the field.

Cavendish published 14 books on science and several volumes of poetry. Her early theory on matter was that atoms corresponded to the accepted four elements. Fire atoms were sharp, earth atoms were square, water atoms were round, and air atoms were long. Disease resulted when atoms fought each other or when the four types were imbalanced. Although most scientists disregarded her work, she was invited to a session of the Royal Society of London in 1667.

Mary Agnes Meara Chase (1869–1963)
Botanist, illustrator

AGNES CHASE'S INTEREST IN BOTANY MAY HAVE BEEN sparked by a wildflower guide that she once read with her nephew. It certainly didn't come from formal schooling. Growing up in Chicago, she left school after eighth grade to work. In 1888 she married William Chase, but his death the next year left her poorer than ever. She supported herself at odd jobs.

One day, while collecting plants, Chase met Reverend Ellsworth Hill, an expert on mosses. He taught her about local plants and how to use a microscope. Chase illustrated his publications from 1898 to 1903 and also made drawings for the Field Museum of Natural History in Chicago. In 1903 she took a position at the United States Department of Agriculture Bureau of Plant Industry in Washington, D.C.

At the bureau, Albert Spear Hitchcock became her mentor. Eventually, she succeeded him as principal scientist in charge of systemic agrostology, the study of grasses. During one journey to Brazil, she collected 4,500 plant species—she collected over 12,000 during her career. Officially she retired in 1939, but she was active at the bureau for decades afterward.

Chase was also a prominent social activist. She protested with suffragist Alice Paul and supported the NAACP and the Women's International League for Peace and Freedom, among other organizations.

Evelyn Lucy Cheesman (1881–1969)
Entomologist, explorer

EVELYN CHEESMAN, THE DAUGHTER OF A WEALTHY British shopkeeper, originally wanted to become a veterinary surgeon, but women weren't allowed to attend veterinary school. So she chose the

Adventures of an Entomologist

In the Galápagos Islands, Evelyn Cheesman once got stuck in a Nephila spiderweb, the exceedingly strong fibers of which drape from the trees: "All around hung spiders of all ages, some near my face. I did not think them handsome any more. Some were jerked out of their meditations and scrambled away, but many were pendant just out of reach of my wild plungings and seemed interested in this new form of entertainment." She finally freed herself with a nail file.

EVELYN CHEESMAN,
Things Worth While

closest job to a veterinarian that was open to her, working as a "canine nurse." World War I began, and she volunteered for the government as a typist in London. She took refuge during her lunch hours at the Natural History Museum's insect department.

Her life took a welcome turn when she met Professor Maxwell Lefroy, curator of the Insect House at the Regents Park Zoo. By 1918 she was not only working for him, she was attending his entomology class at Imperial College. Five years later, she was invited on her first research expedition, to the Galápagos Islands and New Guinea.

Cheesman spent the next 30 years traveling and exploring the tropical rain forests of Southeast Asia and was often accompanied only by native guides. During her career, she collected 40,000 insects, many of which she catalogued herself at the British Museum. She published several books, including *Things Worth While* (1957), which expresses the joy she felt for her work. Cheesman was 74 years old when she went on her final expedition.

May Edward Chinn (1896–1980)
Physician

Dr. May Chinn's father was a former slave, and her mother was a Chickahominy Indian. A talented pianist, she started out as a music major at Teacher's College of Columbia University but later changed her focus to science. She continued performing in concerts in New York City, though, and she socialized with a number of famous musicians, including Paul Robeson.

In 1926 May Chinn became the first African American women to earn a medical degree from the Bellevue Hospital Medical College. During her internship, she was also the first woman doctor to accompany an ambulance team from Harlem Hospital. After 1928, Chinn practiced at Edgecombe Sanitarium, a facility that was run by African

Americans. At the same time, she turned to cancer research and spent 12 years working with George Papanicolaou, the inventor of the "pap smear," a test used to detect cervical cancer in its early stages.

Chinn was devoted to her community, often adjusting her fees so patients could afford to see her. She worked in many clinics and in three state-funded day-care centers in Harlem. Even after her retirement in 1977, she continued working for medical and social service agencies until her death.

Cornelia Maria Clapp (1849–1934)
Zoologist

It is not coincidental that so many women zoologists graduated from Mount Holyoke College. In the 1870s Susan Bowen, a gifted teacher, helped direct Cornelia Clapp's interest to zoology. Clapp specialized in the field and began a tradition that lasted nearly a century, in which women professors encouraged their talented students to pursue further study and then come back to teach.

Cornelia Clapp studied mathematics and gymnastics at Mount Holyoke, but a colleague, Lydia Shattuck, urged her to indulge her interest in science. In 1874 she enrolled in the School of Natural History, which was established by Louis Agassiz on Penikese Island off the Massachusetts coast. One of the few places where women could pursue an interest in science at the time, the coeducational school helped male students learn that women were competent colleagues. Clapp's influence was also important at another research and teaching institution that supported women scientists, the Marine Biological Laboratories at Woods Hole, Massachusetts.

Clapp earned two Ph.D.s, the first from Syracuse University in 1889 and a second from the University of Chicago in 1896. But until her retirement in 1916, she could often be found teaching and researching at Mount Holyoke. An inspiring and well-loved teacher for 44 years, she was a significant force in the establishment of the zoology department there. When the college built a new science laboratory in 1923, it was named for her.

Edith Jane Claypole (1870–1915)
Physiologist, pathologist

Agnes Claypole Moody (1870–1954)
Zoologist

EDITH AND AGNES CLAYPOLE WERE IDENTICAL twins who had many of the same interests. They were strongly influenced by their parents, who educated them at home. Both women earned degrees from Buchtel College in Ohio, where their father taught geology. They also worked with him at the Throop Polytechnic Institute (later called California Institute of Technology). Edith was an instructor in geology and biology, while Agnes assisted her father and took charge of his department after his death.

The twins also studied and worked together away from their parents. Both earned master's degrees from Cornell University in New York. They taught together at Wellesley College in Massachusetts, then returned to Cornell. Edith became acting head of the zoology department, and Agnes was the first woman to teach the lab courses required of all students. Although Agnes had a Ph.D. from the University of Chicago, she was not appointed a full professor at Cornell. That position was not open to women until 1911.

Eventually the sisters' paths diverged. Agnes married Dr. Robert Moody, whose mother, Dr. Mary Blair Moody, was the first woman elected to the American Association of Anatomists. She went with him to San Francisco, where he taught. She worked at Mills

College in Oakland from 1918 to 1923. Edith began studying medicine at Cornell and completed her degree at the University of Los Angeles, specializing in pathology. She died of typhoid fever contracted while researching the bacteria that caused the illness.

Harriet Clisby (1830–1931)
Physician, feminist

HARRIET CLISBY WAS BORN IN ENGLAND BUT spent most of her childhood on a farm in Australia. When she was 17 years old, she joined the Swedenborgian New Church, forming a lifelong interest in moral, spiritual, and bodily health.

Clisby's first career was in journalism. In 1861 she was a founder of *The Interpreter*, the first Australian magazine published by women. But her goals changed after she encountered the writings of Elizabeth Blackwell, the first woman doctor in America. She was immediately inspired to follow Blackwell's example.

After receiving tutoring in anatomy, Clisby moved to London to become a nurse at Guy's Hospital. When a friend offered to pay her tuition at the Medical College and Hospital for Women in New York, Clisby moved again. She got her M.D. in 1865 and opened a practice in Boston, Massachusetts. In 1871 she founded the Women's Educational and Industrial Union, an organization similar to the YMCA. She eventually retired to Geneva, Switzerland, and remained an active feminist until her death at the age of 100.

Rebecca Cole (1846–1922)
Physician

REBECCA COLE WAS RAISED IN PHILADELPHIA, where she was an outstanding student at the Institute for Colored Youth. In 1867 she became the first African American woman to graduate from the Woman's Medical College of Pennsylvania and only the second black female doctor in the country.

Cole began her career at the New York Infirmary for Women and Children, founded by Drs. Emily and Elizabeth Blackwell and Dr. Marie Zakrzewska. While there, she worked as a "sanitary visitor" to poor neighborhoods, teaching families the basics of hygiene, infant care, and general health.

Social and political causes were also important to Cole. She was superintendent of a government shelter for children and elderly women in Washington, D.C. In Philadelphia, where she settled, she ran a homeless shelter. In 1873 she helped to establish a Women's Directory Center that provided legal and medical aid. A respected physician in her community, Cole's career spanned half a century.

Gerty Theresa Radnitz Cori (1896–1957)
Biochemist

OUR BODIES CAN CREATE ENERGY USING FOOD. This process, called metabolism, occurs in the cells, where glycogen, a compound formed from the carbohydrates we eat, is changed into sugars the body can use. Knowing how glycogen works helps us understand normal human metabolism. It also helps explain diseases such as diabetes, where the process does not work properly.

Gerty Radnitz Cori and her husband, Carl, contributed much to our understanding about the way human cells use carbohydrates. A true team,

the couple began researching together in medical school in Prague, Czechoslovakia. When they immigrated to the United States in 1922, Carl was treated very differently from Gerty. They both had medical degrees, but he received prestigious positions and high salaries, while she was only offered work as an assistant biochemist. Gerty was even told she was damaging his career by continuing their collaboration. However, their work on glycogen and their success in synthesizing it in a test tube earned them the 1947 Nobel Prize for medicine.

By the time the Nobel Prize ceremony was held, Gerty Cori had already learned that she had myelosclerosis, an incurable bone disease. However, she and Carl decided not to tell anyone until after receiving the award. She continued researching glycogen and determined its chemical structure in 1954. Carl and Gerty's only child, Carl Thomas, also became a research scientist.

Eva Crane (1912–)
Apiculturist

IN 1942, DURING WORLD WAR II, EVA AND JAMES Crane got married. Because there was a sugar shortage in England, a wedding guest gave them a swarm of honeybees. That gift changed Eva's life. Already a trained scientist, Crane had a Ph.D. in physics from King's College in London. She began researching bees and discovered there was little organized communication among the bee scientists of the world. So began her journey into the world of apiculture.

By 1949 Crane had become director of the International Bee Research Association. The next year, she became editor of *Bee World* and transformed it into a respected scientific journal. Her first book, *Honey: A Comprehensive Study*, was published in 1975. She has studied her subject from every angle, including looking back through millennia to write *The Archaeology of Bee Keeping* (1983).

To establish contacts Crane has often traveled abroad. She helped establish programs to teach beekeeping in Vietnam and visited honey hunters in Nepal, whose bees build their nests in the steep, rocky Himalayas. She has received many awards, including being appointed an officer in the Order of the British Empire by Queen Elizabeth.

Maria Dalle Donne (1778–1842)

Physician

MARIA DALLE DONNE WAS ONE OF SEVERAL Italian women of the 18th century who earned a medical degree. Italy, unlike other countries, did not forbid women from attending universities. As a child, Dalle Donne's intelligence was recognized by her uncle, who provided tutors to educate her. In 1799 she received a degree in philosophy and medicine from the University of Bologna, along with many honors from the faculty.

Dalle Donne's intelligence and capabilities impressed many, including the Italian-born emperor of France, Napoleon Bonaparte. Prospero Ranuzzi, a philanthropist who was especially interested in science, gave her his collection of medical instruments and books. In 1804 Dalle Donne became director of the Bologna School of Midwives. She was an excellent teacher with high standards, who accepted many talented students, even though they could not afford tuition. She consistently tried to improve poor and sometimes dangerous midwifery practices through education. One of her goals was to send well-trained midwives to villages where doctors were not available.

Frances Theresa Densmore (1867–1957)

Ethnomusicologist, anthropologist

AS A CHILD IN RED WING, MINNESOTA, FRANCES Densmore often heard the music of the Sioux tribe living near her home. The study and preservation of Native American songs would eventually become her life's work. But first she took a traditional path of music education and teaching, first at Oberlin College in Ohio, and then in Boston, Massachusetts. She wrote to Alice Cunningham Fletcher, an anthropologist, about her interests in American Indian music and received a positive and encouraging reply.

Densmore made her first field trip in 1905 with her sister Margaret, who would eventually become her constant traveling companion and assistant. Early in her career Densmore transcribed music by listening, but she soon found that using a phonograph was the best way to record songs. She was particularly interested in the cultural context of songs, especially the use of music in Native American medical practice. Her method was to record a variety of songs and make observations about daily activities. She paid her singers in cash and thanked them in her publications.

Densmore's caring and straightforward style combined with her commitment to preserving Native American culture brought her honor in the Sioux tribe. They adopted her as a daughter and gave her the name Two White Buffalo Woman. Some anthropologists feel her work was superficial, but most acknowledge that she was a pioneer in the field of ethnomusicology.

Frances Densmore records while a Native American man sings.

Lydia Maria Adams De Witt
(1859–1928)
Pathologist

DR. LYDIA DE WITT TAUGHT IN MICHIGAN PUBLIC schools before she decided to pursue a career in medicine. She earned her M.D. at the University of Michigan when she was 39. Again she taught, this time at the university level. In 1912 she joined the research staff of the Otho S.A. Sprague Memorial Institute at the University of Chicago. There she looked for chemical treatments for tuberculosis, a bacterial disease that affects the lungs. Dr. Paul Ehrlich had found a treatment for syphilis using dyes linked with toxic metals. De Witt decided to try the same strategy.

She approached the problem by finding out which types of dyes would stain the bacteria that caused tuberculosis. Then, in collaboration with chemists, she tried linking those dyes with gold, copper, and mercury. The combinations were tested on laboratory animals.

De Witt was not able to find a treatment for tuberculosis. But her research provided the model that led to the discovery of one. Well-respected in her field, she received an honorary degree from the University of Michigan in 1914. She is remembered as a meticulous and talented researcher.

Gladys Rowena Henry Dick
(1881–1963)
Physician, microbiologist

GLADYS DICK AND HER HUSBAND, GEORGE Frederick, were doctors who worked together to research the disease scarlet fever. They met at the University of Chicago, married in 1914, and went on to work together at the John R. McCormick Memorial Institute for Infectious Diseases. In addition to her medical research, Gladys was active in the welfare of adopted children. She helped found the Cradle Society, one of America's first adoption agencies. She and George adopted two babies in 1930.

During the 1920s scarlet fever was a frequent and serious childhood affliction. A rash would appear after a sore throat and high fever. Many children suffered serious complications, such as kidney problems and rheumatic fever. Twenty-five percent of those who got the disease died from it.

Gladys and George's research on scarlet fever was extensive. Their most significant contribution was determining that the same bacteria that caused strep throat also caused scarlet fever. These bacteria, which were of the *streptococcus* type, produced a toxin that caused a rash. The Dicks used that information to develop a skin test that could determine whether an individual child was susceptible. The "Dick test" was very important until antibiotics became available in the 1940s and made it possible to cure scarlet fever. Gladys and George were nominated for the Nobel Prize in medicine in 1925, but no prize was awarded in their field that year.

June Etta Downey
(1875–1932)
Experimental psychologist

COMING FROM A FAMILY OF PIONEERS ON AMERICA'S western frontier, June Etta Downey was a pioneer in the field of psychology. A native of Laramie, Wyoming, she already had a master's degree in psychology when she began teaching English at the University of Wyoming in 1898. Her interest in psychology developed further during a summer course at Cornell University in 1901. After earning her Ph.D. at the University of Chicago, she returned to Wyoming in 1908 and was appointed head of the university's psychology department. No other woman had yet occupied such a high position at a state university.

Many psychologists of the time focused on measuring intelligence. Downey tried to assess the whole personality. She devised a new type of personality test, and although it is not still used, it formed the basis for similar tools. She was also interested in creativity, handwriting analysis, and right- and left-handedness.

Downey was a model teacher and counselor. Remaining true to her early love of literature, she wrote fiction as well as scientific works. In 1929 she and Margaret Floy Washburn became the first women ever granted membership to the Society of Experimental Psychology.

Cornelia Mitchell Downs (1892–1987)
Bacteriologist

WHEN THE SPECIAL POSITION OF SUMMERFIELD Distinguished Professor of Bacteriology was created at the University of Kansas, its founder said a woman would never deserve to be honored with the title. He was proved wrong in 1972, when Dr. Cora Downs gleefully accepted the appointment. She had started at the university as an undergraduate, earned her Ph.D. in 1924, and spent most of her long, successful career there.

Downs's specialty was the study of tularemia, or "rabbit fever." The many wild rabbits in Kansas had provided free food during the Depression. But some of the animals carried diseases, and rabbit fever was especially unpleasant. Its symptoms included body aches, swollen lymph glands, and sores that didn't heal.

In 1930 Downs got a sample of *Pasteurella tularensis*—the bacterium that causes the disease—from a sore on a rabbit hunter's finger. Such samples can often be made into vaccines, but this bacterial strain could not. After much experimentation Downs succeeded in her search in the late 1940s, when she began working with Russian scientists who had collected bacteria that did yield an effective vaccine.

Dr. Downs is also remembered for her work on a technique known as fluorescent antibody staining. She formulated a stable dye with which to stain serum for examination under the microscope. Her article about it, published in the *American Journal of Pathology* in 1958, became an important reference for scientists.

Marie Josefina Durocher (1809–1895)
Obstetrician

MARIE DUROCHER WAS BORN IN PARIS, BUT WHEN she was eight years old, her family immigrated to Brazil. She married and might never have pursued a career if her husband had not died. But by the time she was 24, Marie found herself alone with two small children to support.

Durocher began studying obstetrics at the new medical school in Rio de Janeiro. In 1834 she became the first student to receive a diploma from the school, and was one of Latin America's first female health professionals. Durocher was influenced by such practitioners as the Frenchwomen Louyse Bourgeois and Marie Boivin.

Durocher practiced medicine in Brazil for over 60 years. She usually dressed in men's clothes rather than struggle with the long, cumbersome skirts that were fashionable at the time. She was a well-respected doctor and, in 1871, was elected to Brazil's National Academy of Medicine.

Sylvia Alice Earle (1935–)
Marine biologist, environmentalist, deep-sea explorer

IN 1979 SYLVIA EARLE PUT ON A SPECIAL *JIM* SUIT and plunged 1,250 feet (381 m) into the ocean, breaking the world record for deepest ocean dive. She then spent over two hours studying the marine organisms she saw. Many would argue that the dive was as risky as the Apollo moon landing ten years earlier, but Earle received little attention.

Wanting to explore even deeper, Earle founded Deep Ocean Engineering with Graham Hawkes, a designer of the *Jim* suit. One of their early projects was Deep Rover, a submersible marine vehicle that could carry one person to a depth of 3,000 feet (914 m). During the 1990s she worked with a team of

"A science-fiction thriller could not have been more bizarre than my recent encounters with the blue-flashing coral whiskers and some of their associates: huge deep-sea rays hovering like enormous butterflies a few feet from the sea floor, a full-grown 18-inch-long shark with glowing green eyes, dozens of long-clawed red crabs, clinging to a lush shrub of pink coral, luminous jelly-creatures, and a slender silver-black lanternfish spangled with a lateral row of blue lights—the first I had ever seen alive, in its own realm."

SYLVIA EARLE, on her journey
in *Jim, Sea Change,* 1995

Japanese scientists on a project that would allow divers to travel over ten times deeper.

Earle wants the public both to enjoy and respect the oceans. She studied the devastating effects of the oil spill from the Exxon ship, *Valdez,* in 1989. The next year, she was appointed the first female chief scientist of the National Oceanic and Atmospheric Administration. But she became frustrated with the government's policies and left after 18 months, convinced that she could do more good with her own projects.

A teacher and author as well as a respected scientist and daring explorer, Earle has received many honors and awards. Perhaps the most appropriate recognition of her work has been the naming of two sea organisms for her, the sea urchin *Diadema sylvie,* and the plant *Pilinia earli.*

Alice Eastwood (1859–1953)
Botanist

ALICE EASTWOOD'S BOTANICAL WORK BENEFITED gardeners, hikers, and plant-enthusiasts, as well as scientists. She was active in encouraging public interest in botany and promoting preservation of plant species. She wrote and illustrated over 300 articles and books.

Eastwood was born in Toronto, Canada, but lived in many places after her mother died when she was six. First she was sent to live with her uncle, a doctor who taught her the Latin names of plants. At age eight, she went to live in a convent and learned to garden from a French priest. When she was 14, she returned to her father and two siblings, who had since moved to Colorado. She was valedictorian of her high school class in 1879 and spent the next decade teaching and learning as much about botany as she could.

In 1892 Eastwood moved to San Francisco, where Katherine Brandegee, the curator of the California Academy of Sciences, had offered her a job as an assistant. Two years later she became curator herself and remained until her retirement in 1949.

Eastwood enjoyed the opportunities her job gave her to travel and collect plants. Her love for the Academy's botany collection was exemplified by her actions during the 1906 earthquake. As the building went up in flames after the quake, she rushed in and saved the most critical specimens. She went on to restore the collection, adding 340,000 specimens from around the world.

Fannie Hardy Eckstorm (1865–1946)
Folklorist, ornithologist, writer

FANNIE ECKSTORM'S CAREER as a writer, ornithologist, folklorist, and expert on Native American culture was shaped by her childhood in Brewer, Maine. Her family socialized with members of the local Penobscot Indian settlement. Her father, a fur trader, knew the area well, and she was his companion for many journeys in the woods. He taught her about observing and recording the habits of animals.

Eckstorm's work in ornithology began when she was at Smith College in Massachusetts, where she founded a student Audubon Society. She went on to write for popular bird magazines, including *Auk* and *Bird-Lore,* and even wrote for children in *The Bird Book* (1901).

Her interest in Native American culture may have been most influenced by a canoe trip with her father through the wilderness of the Penobscot waters and the Nicatowis region. She was probably the first white woman to visit this area. In 1941 she published *Indian Place-Names of the Penobscot Valley and the Maine Coast*, describing the landscape as viewed from a canoe. Her final book, *Old John Neptune and Other Maine Indian Shamans* (1945), reflected her acceptance of the idea of clairvoyance, the ability to perceive things that aren't visible or material. Her research and writings have helped preserve the history of Native Americans in Maine.

Tilly Edinger (1897–1967)
Paleontologist

D R. TILLY EDINGER WAS A WELL-RESPECTED paleontologist at the Senckenberg Museum in Frankfurt, Germany. Her family had lived in the city for generations, and, even after World War II began, she had hoped to stay in her hometown. But Edinger was Jewish. For five years, with the support of her colleagues, she crept into the museum through a side entrance and worked in an unmarked office. Finally in 1939 she had to leave.

Edinger moved to Massachusetts in 1940 and began a career at Harvard University's Museum of Comparative Zoology. Her specialty, in which she was

a pioneer, was paleoneurology, the study of mammal fossil brains. By filling a fossilized skull with plaster, she was able to make a cast that showed how the surface of the brain had looked. She analyzed casts from different ages to track the evolution of the brain. Her findings suggested that evolution was more complex than the "ladder" from simpler life forms up through humans that most scientists envisioned. Her book, *The Evolution of the Horse Brain* (1948), and more than 60 papers describe her theories.

Dr. Edinger was one of the most important paleontologists of the 20th century. She was also beloved for her warm, spirited personality and, as a deaf scientist, inspired many people. She was president of the Society of Vertebrate Paleontology in 1963 and received honorary degrees from several universities.

Rosa Smith Eigenmann (1858–1947)
Ichthyologist

A LTHOUGH YOUNG ROSA SMITH ENROLLED IN business college, her real interest was in the wildlife that inhabited her home state of California. Studying on her own, she discovered a new species of fish and read a paper about it in 1880, at a meeting of the San Diego Society of Natural History—where she was the first female member. The ichthyologist David Starr Jordan was impressed. He convinced her to attend Indiana University, where he taught, and included her in a select group of students he took traveling to conduct fishery surveys.

In 1887 Rosa married Carl H. Eigenmann, another of Jordan's best students. Together they worked at Harvard University studying the collection of South American fish. Then they collaborated in San Diego at a research station Carl established. Rosa published 15 papers with her husband and 20 on her own, becoming the first recognized woman ichthyologist.

The Eigenmanns returned to Indiana, where Carl became a zoology professor, in 1891. Rosa soon left her career to raise their five children, although she continued editing Carl's work. She was realistic about the difficulties women faced, balancing family responsibilities with a scientific career. Even so, she did not agree that this meant they should lower their expectations of themselves. "Woman should be judged by the same standard as her brother," she said, "Her work must not simply be well done *for a woman*."

Joycelyn Elders (1933–)
Physician, Surgeon General of the United States

JOYCELYN ELDERS, THE DAUGHTER OF SHARECROPPERS, grew up in the town of Schaal, Arkansas. She attended Philander Smith College in Little Rock on a scholarship and met a doctor for the first time during her freshman year. Soon she had chosen medicine as her career. She went to the University of Arkansas Medical School, where she was one of only three black students, and graduated in 1960.

Elders became a respected pediatric endocrinologist, a specialist in children's glandular diseases. In 1987 Governor Bill Clinton made her director of the Arkansas Department of Health. Her strong, politically controversial opinions soon became clear. To combat teenage pregnancy, she established health clinics in schools. Conservative religious groups opposed her vigorously; only four of the 24 clinics were allowed to distribute condoms.

In 1993 Bill Clinton, by then president, nominated Elders to succeed Antonia Novello as surgeon general. Again, her outspoken views brought her trouble. In addition to sex education and birth control, Elders supported abortion rights, strict gun control, and said she would consider legalizing certain drugs. Many people, particularly members of the Republican party, were scandalized. The furor grew until, in 1994, the President asked Dr. Elders to resign.

Gertrude Belle Elion (1918–)
Pharmacologist

GERTRUDE ELION BECAME INTERESTED IN MEDICAL research after her grandfather died from stomach cancer. She majored in chemistry at Hunter College in New York City, and graduated at age 19 with honors. But research laboratories were reluctant to hire even such a qualified woman. Then World War II arrived. Many men left their jobs, and positions became available. For a time Elion worked at a quality control lab, where her duties included monitoring the color of mayonnaise. At last, in 1944, she was hired by George Hitchings, a biochemist at the Burroughs Wellcome Research Laboratories. Starting out as Hitchings's assistant, Elion became his collaborator.

Working as a team, Hitchings and Elion followed new research methods. While other scientists tried several different drugs on animals with a disease, Hitchings and Elion focused on the biochemistry of cells. First, they compared the growth of harmful cells—such as cancers, bacteria, and viruses—to the growth of healthy cells. Using this information, they searched for compounds that would affect only the malfunctions in the cells' chemistry. They developed treatments for several conditions, including herpes and organ-transplant rejection. They created drugs that helped fight childhood leukemia. AZT, a drug used to treat people with AIDS, could not have been developed without the foundations they laid.

WHO

One of the activities that kept Gertrude Elion busy in the 1980s after her retirement was her work on malaria for the World Health Organization. A special arm of the United Nations, WHO was founded in 1948 and is based in Geneva, Switzerland. Its scope is broad: the organization's avowed mission is complete physical and mental health for *all* people. Numerous WHO programs exist to promote research, distribute information, provide education, and sponsor medical care. Largely because of WHO's work, smallpox, a devastating disease, is considered to have been eradicated—the last documented case was in 1977.

Elion retired in 1983, but remained active as a consultant, and recognition of her work even increased. Elion and Hitchings shared the 1988 Nobel Prize for physiology or medicine with the English pharmacologist Sir James Whyte Black. In 1991 Elion received the National Medal of Science and was inducted into the National Inventors' Hall of Fame.

Dorothea Leporin Erxleben (1715–1762)
Physician

DOROTHEA LEPORIN AND HER BROTHER, CHRISTIAN, learned Latin, science, and medicine with their physician father. Both wanted to become doctors. However, German law required that Christian serve in the military, and women weren't permitted to earn medical degrees. Dorothea wrote a letter to King Frederick the Great addressing both issues. As a result, she was given special permission to attend the University of Halle, and Christian was freed from military service so that he could start his studies there, too.

Dorothea's plans were interrupted by her marriage to Johann Christian Erxleben. Soon she was mother to four children from her husband's previous marriage and then had four of her own. Meanwhile, she studied independently and tended the poor—until three local doctors accused her of practicing illegally. Luckily, her admission to the university was still valid. In 1754 Erxleben became the first woman to earn an M.D. from a German school.

Two written works by Erxleben are known. In the 1700s, bad-tasting medicine was believed to be most effective, an idea she challenged in her doctoral thesis. She also wrote *Rational Thoughts on an Education of the Fair Sex* (1749). Erxleben died early, at age 47, having practiced medicine for only eight years.

Alice Catherine Evans (1881–1975)
Bacteriologist

BRUCELLOSIS, OR "UNDULANT FEVER," WAS A troublesome disease. With symptoms that included headaches, pains, and general discomfort, it was difficult to diagnose because it resembled many

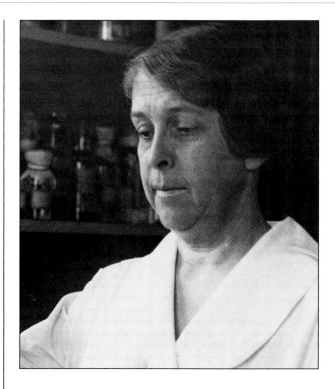

other ailments. By the early 1900s, brucellosis had been traced to milk, but just exactly how milk from apparently healthy cows became contaminated was still a mystery.

Alice Evans, a bacteriologist working for the United States government, solved the mystery, but scientists didn't believe her for several years. In 1917 Evans announced that she had found similarities between *Bacillus abortus*, a type of bacteria that caused a disease in cows, and *Micrococcus melitensis*, a kind of bacteria found in raw goat's milk and was known to harm humans if they drank it. She proposed that pasteurization of cow's milk—heating it to kill the bacteria—would fix the problem, just as it had with the goat's milk. Neither the scientific community nor dairy farmers wanted to hear that.

Evans continued her research, even after she accidentally contracted brucellosis herself (she suffered until penicillin became available in the 1940s). Gradually, scientists repeated her experiments and began to accept her theories. A new genus of bacteria, *Brucellus*, was created in 1920 to include the two organisms Evans had studied. In 1928 Evans became the first woman president of the Society of Bacteriologists. Still, it was not until the 1930s that all milk sold in America was required to be pasteurized.

Fabiola (4th century)
Physician

Fabiola, a Roman aristocrat, grew up in a society that worshiped many different gods. She converted to Christianity, a relatively new religion at the time, after leaving an abusive first husband. She married again, but was soon widowed. Convinced that this was her punishment for divorcing her first husband and for a youth spent in frivolity, she devoted herself to charitable works.

Fabiola learned of a man named Jerome, a devout scholar and Christian leader who was later declared a saint. She traveled to Bethlehem to be near him and joined a group of his women disciples who practiced medicine and helped the poor. Returning to Italy, she used her fortune to establish monasteries and, in 390, founded a hospital at Porto with her friends Paula and Pammachius. There, they treated people who were rejected by other doctors because they were too poor or too sick. Fabiola is thought to have performed surgeries and was known for her sympathetic manner. She is considered a saint by Roman Catholics, for whom such Christian converts as Fabiola are pioneers.

Margaret Clay Ferguson (1863–1951)
Botanist

It took 50 years for technology to confirm botanist Margaret Clay Ferguson's theory about *Petunia* plant inheritance. The genus *Petunia* was assumed to pass on characteristics, such as flower color and petal arrangement, in a predictable pattern. But she disagreed, theorizing that the genes that controlled certain traits were changeable. Using her ideas, she reclassified the plants of that genus into new taxonomic categories. And two decades after her death, she was proved right. Ferguson's focus on plant genetics helped establish botany as a legitimate science, rather than just a hobby involving plant collection.

Ferguson was only 14 when she began teaching at public schools. From 1888 to 1891, she studied as a special student at Wellesley College in Massachusetts, and she was hired there as a botany instructor in 1893. From then on, except for a few years spent earning a Ph.D. from Cornell University, she made her career at Wellesley. Her influence as an educator was remarkable. Her botany courses included chemistry, physics, and genetics. She emphasized lab work and encouraged her students to research plant growth, physiology, and genetics. She even modernized the facilities at the college, overseeing the building of two greenhouses. Under Ferguson's guidance, the Wellesley botany department became one of the best in the country.

Lady Amalia Coutsouris Fleming (1909–1986)
Bacteriologist, political activist

Amalia Coutsouris studied medicine at the University of Athens, where she specialized in bacteriology. Receiving her M.D. in 1938, she took a job at the city hospital. Almost immediately, World War II began. Horrified by the Nazis, who occupied Greece in 1941, she joined the resistance, forging identity cards and sheltering refugees until she was betrayed. She spent the last months of the war in prison. Once freed, she moved to London to work at the Wright-Fleming Institute of Microbiology.

Amalia collaborated with Sir Alexander Fleming, the Nobel prize-winning discoverer of penicillin, on

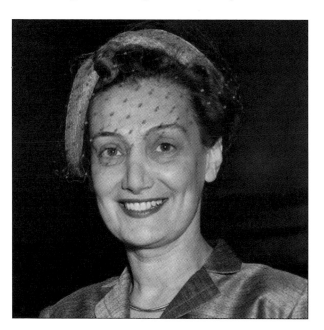

several projects concerning antibiotics, especially one called streptomycin, which is effective in treating tuberculosis. She stayed at the institute for four years and returned to Athens in 1951, but only briefly. The next year, while Fleming was in Greece for a conference, he proposed. They married in 1953 and lived in London. Amalia was devastated when the elderly Fleming died only two years later.

In 1967 Amalia retired from the institute and went home to Greece, just as the government was overthrown by military forces. Again, she spoke out against repression. This time she was world-famous, and the authorities were hesitant to take action. She was imprisoned briefly and deported in 1971. A democracy was established in 1975, and Lady Fleming was able to spend her last years in her homeland.

Alice Cunningham Fletcher (1838–1923)
Anthropologist, reformer

IN THE LATE 1870S, ALICE FLETCHER, AN ACTIVIST who supported such causes as temperance, visited the Peabody Museum in Cambridge, Massachusetts, which was run by F.W. Putnam. The experience sparked what would become a lifelong

Alice Fletcher in the field

interest in anthropology. Soon she began researching Native American culture, with a focus on music.

Fletcher often collaborated with Francis La Flesche, a member of the Omaha and the brother of Dr. Susan La Flesche Picotte and the activist Susette La Flesche. He became her unofficially adopted son. Among the works they published together was the respected study *The Omaha Tribe* (1911). Fletcher's writings made her one of a small number of women welcomed in male scientific circles. She became vice-president of the American Association for the Advancement of Science in 1896 and helped found the American Anthropological Association in 1902.

Her reform efforts on behalf of Native Americans, though well-intentioned, are not as highly regarded as her anthropological work. She lobbied for the Dawes Act of 1887, which parceled out reservation lands to individuals. Fletcher's focus, now seen as misguided, was to try to assure Indians' survival by encouraging them to adopt white values and lifestyles.

Dian Fossey (1932–1985)
Primatologist

DIAN FOSSEY'S SUCCESS IN STUDYING MOUNTAIN gorillas had much to do with her ability to walk, vocalize, and eat like them. Gorillas usually hide from people, but Fossey gained their trust by imitating them and eventually was able to observe the activities of 51 gorillas.

Fossey, a San Francisco native, always loved animals. She studied veterinary science briefly and became a skilled horseback rider. Above all, she was fascinated by mountain gorillas. In 1963, during a vacation to Tanzania, she introduced herself to paleontologist Louis Leakey, who was impressed by her determination. In 1966 Leakey sought out Fossey at her home in Kentucky and persuaded her to make a long-term study of the apes. For most of the next two decades she lived in Africa, although she spent time in England studying zoology at Cambridge University and also taught at Cornell University in New York.

The climate and work conditions at Fossey's camp were harsh, and the political situation was tense. The area belonged to three nations, Rwanda, Zaire, and Uganda. Poachers wanted to kill gorillas for trade or capture them for zoos. Fossey tried to stop them by stealing their weapons and destroying

traps. She began to publicize the situation in 1978, after a gorilla in her group was killed, and in 1983 she published a book, *Gorillas in the Mist*. Her outspokenness may have led to her murder on December 26, 1985. The Karisoke Research Centre, which she established, continues her work.

Lydia Folger Fowler (1822–1879)
Physician, educator, health-care reformer

SUPPORTING AND EDUCATING WOMEN WAS AT THE heart of Lydia Fowler's work. She began lecturing to women while traveling with her husband, Lorenzo Niles Fowler, an expert on phrenology. Today phrenology is not an accepted science, but at that time it was believed that the shape of a person's skull could be analyzed to determine character and personality. Lydia Fowler expanded her lectures, adding information about women's physiology, anatomy, and health. In 1874 she published two books, *Familiar Lessons on Phrenology* and *Familiar Lessons on Physiology*.

Fowler's work soon inspired her to pursue a medical career. She was one of five women to enroll at the first coeducational medical school in the United States, the Central Medical College in Syracuse, New York, in the year it was founded. In

1850 she became the country's second woman doctor after Elizabeth Blackwell. She worked at the college and eventually became a professor of midwifery and diseases of women and children.

In addition to her medical career, Lydia Fowler continued her support of women's rights. She was secretary for the national women's rights conventions in 1852 and 1853. Her novel, *Nora, the Lost and Redeemed* (1863), supported temperance and a woman's right to become a doctor. The Fowlers moved to London in 1863. There Lydia focused on lecturing and writing, providing a valuable service to the many women looking for clear and honest information about their health.

Rosalind Franklin (1921–1958)
X-ray crystallographer, DNA researcher

DNA, OR DEOXYRIBONUCLEIC ACID, IS THE compound in our cells that controls inherited characteristics. A person has ten fingers, for example, because his or her DNA contains directions for that trait to develop. The 1962 Nobel Prize was awarded to James Watson, Francis Crick, and Maurice Wilkins for discovering the structure of DNA. Unfortunately Rosalind Franklin, whose X-ray photographs of the compound made that discovery possible, had died four years earlier from cancer.

It isn't clear whether Franklin would have shared in the Nobel Prize even if she had been alive. Although the men used her results and photographs, they treated her terribly. Wilkins, her supervisor at King's College in London, showed her research to Watson and Crick without her permission. In Wilkins's book, *The Double Helix* (1968), he describes Franklin as a lab assistant and calls her Rosy.

Born into an upper middle-class Jewish family in London, Franklin graduated from Newnham College, Cambridge, in 1941. After a difficult time working with the chemist Ronald Norrish, who did not want her in his lab, she moved to Paris. There, at the Central Laboratory of Chemical Sciences, she made great progress using X rays to understand molecular structure. She was invited to King's College to build X-ray equipment for molecular research. This led to her DNA discoveries. Although her work was going well, she left King's College because of the way she was treated and turned to virology research. Her findings have contributed much to scientists' knowledge of the genetics of viruses. Sadly, as in her life, there has been little recognition of Rosalind Franklin since her death.

Anna Freud (1895–1982)

Psychoanalyst

ANNA FREUD, THE YOUNGEST CHILD OF SIGMUND Freud, developed the field of childhood psychoanalysis. She was a schoolteacher for several years before she began to follow in her father's footsteps. In 1922, after publishing her first paper, she became a formal member of the Vienna Psycho-Analytical Society. The following year she opened her own practice. The Nazis invaded Austria in 1938, forcing the Freuds, who were Jewish, to flee to London, where Sigmund soon died.

Anna Freud was interested in examining the ways consciousness—the *ego*—worked to protect a person from anxiety and fear. An early trend in psychoanalysis was to concentrate on the patient's unconscious needs and desires—the *id*—but she

wanted to achieve a more balanced view. She felt that the *ego* was adaptable and that a patient could learn to control negative reactions to fearful and anxiety-provoking situations. She also felt that childhood psychoanalysis should differ from the process adults went through. She created a diagnostic test that assessed children's mental development.

During World War II, Freud directed the Hampstead War Nursery for children who had been separated from their parents. It was later replaced by the Hampstead Child Therapy Course and Clinic. She also continued to make contributions to child psychology. Her accessible, elegant writing style has made her work popular with both doctors and the general public.

Elizabeth Smith Friedman (1892–1980)

Cryptologist

ONE OF THE MOST UNUSUAL SCIENCES IS cryptology, the study of encoded meanings in communications. Elizabeth and William Friedman were experts in this field. In 1915, newly graduated from Michigan's Hillsdale College with a degree in English, Elizabeth was hired by George Fabyan, founder of the Riverbank Laboratories in Illinois. The eccentric Fabyan suspected that William Shakespeare hadn't written the plays and poems ascribed to him. He believed another writer of Shakespeare's day, Sir Francis Bacon, was the true author, and that a coded message in the texts would confirm this. Her job was to break the code. William, a geneticist hired for a different project, began to help. They married in 1917.

As part of their work, the Friedmans learned all about codes. Soon the government started sending intercepted messages for them to decipher. In 1921 they moved to Washington, D.C., where William joined the War Department. As a special agent to the Coast Guard, Elizabeth broke over 12,000 radio messages sent by people trying to smuggle liquor into the country during Prohibition. During World War II, she deciphered messages from German spies for the Office of Strategic Services. The pair never forgot the way they met and eventually wrote a book, *The Shakespearean Ciphers Examined* (1957), in which they planted a coded message: "I did not write the plays. F. Bacon."

Frieda Fromm-Reichmann (1889–1957)
Psychiatrist, psychoanalyst

FRIEDA REICHMANN GREW UP IN A HIGHLY educated Jewish family in Königsberg, East Prussia. At her parents' encouragement, she went to the medical school at Albertus University. She was an excellent student and considered becoming an obstetrician, but thought her size (she was less than five feet tall) might make it difficult. Instead, when she graduated in 1913, she chose psychiatry.

Frieda spent the last half of World War I caring for soldiers with serious brain injuries. After the war, she studied Sigmund Freud's psychoanalytical methods. She married the psychologist Erich Fromm in 1926.

By 1935, with World War II on the horizon, she was divorced and living in the United States. For the rest of her career, she worked at Chestnut Lodge, a sanitarium in Maryland. She concentrated on patients with such severe illnesses as manic-depression or schizophrenia, which many doctors felt would not respond to psychotherapy. But Fromm-Reichmann's compassionate, attentive focus on the individual produced remarkably good results. The popular book *I Never Promised You a Rose Garden* (1964), by Hannah Green, describes a grateful patient's recovery through treatment by Dr. Fromm-Reichmann.

Biruté M. F. Galdikas (1946–)
Primatologist, conservationist

THE INDONESIAN RAIN FORESTS ARE HOT AND humid. There are king cobras, poisonous plants, leeches—and orangutans—which is why Biruté Galdikas has spent most of her time since 1971 on the island of Borneo. She is trying to understand human evolution by studying these "people of the forest," as *orangutan* means in Indonesian.

Galdikas grew up in Toronto, Canada, and earned a degree in anthropology at the University of California at Los Angeles. She had already decided she wanted to study orangutans when she met Dr. Louis Leakey in 1969. Leakey, who also had helped Jane Goodall and Dian Fossey find funding and resources for their research, supported Galdikas, too.

> "When faced with an angry, three-hundred-pound wild adult male orangutan, with an arm span of perhaps eight feet, I try not to react. I force myself to do nothing. Even if the people with me turn and flee, I remain where I am, silent, immobile, expressionless. The orangutan must make a split-second decision: engage me in combat and risk injury, or withdraw into his meditative state and save himself for the real battle. . . . Sometimes facing a wild orangutan male is not altogether different from facing the human forces aligned against him."
>
> BIRUTÉ GALDIKAS
> *Reflections of Eden: My Years with the Orangutans of Borneo*, 1995

Galdikas has spent countless hours observing her subjects. She has confirmed that they are solitary animals, although females sometimes form small social groups. Although the quality of her research is high, some scientists have criticized her for not publishing more. She replies that her more immediate concern is conservation and public awareness. The orangutan population, once estimated at 500,000, has dropped to about 10,000, mostly because of the destruction of their habitat. In 1987 she founded the Orangutan Foundation International to help protect these creatures she has come to know so well.

Rosa Hirschmann Gantt (1875–1935)
Public health administrator, physician

ROSA GANTT EARNED HER M.D. FROM THE MEDICAL College of South Carolina in 1901. An eye, ear, nose, and throat specialist, she opened a private practice. In addition, she devoted much of her energy to promoting public health.

One of Gantt's most significant contributions was the establishment of a "healthmobile" for Spartanburg County in the southern Appalachias. Pellagra, a disease caused by a deficiency of protein and niacin in the diet, was a serious problem. A team made up of a doctor, nurse, dentist, and nutrition worker traveled around the area, explaining what to do about pellagra and providing general check-ups, immunizations, and dental examinations. Within four years, the incidences of pellagra reported annually in Spartanburg County had dropped from 572 cases to 35.

Dr. Gantt used her influence to help women progress in medicine. She was active in the Medical Women's National Association and on the South Carolina Board of Public Welfare. She also worked to promote women's political rights and served as the legislative chair of the South Carolina Equal Suffrage League.

Erna Gibbs (1904–1987)
Medical researcher, electroencephalographer

Erna Leonhardt, born and educated in Germany, immigrated to America after World War I. She found a job as a lab assistant at Harvard Medical School in Boston and even enrolled in medical school. The discrimination she encountered as a student was too discouraging, though. She quit school. Continuing her work in the labs, Erna made herself into an expert, even though she didn't have a degree. She married Frederic Gibbs, a neuropathologist, in 1930.

Together the Gibbses embarked on a study of the seizures that were characteristic of a disease known as epilepsy. Most scientists thought seizures were caused by changes in the amount of blood flowing to the brain. So the scientists measured blood flow during seizures—Erna, with her lab experience, actually took the measurements, a delicate process. They found no correlation. They decided to use an electroencephalograph, or EEG, to figure out what was going on.

The brain constantly generates rhythmical electrical surges, or brain waves. These waves can be measured by an EEG. First the Gibbses devised a more sensitive EEG apparatus by working with scientists who were developing equipment to measure earthquakes. Then they began mapping the changing patterns of brain waves during epileptic seizures. Over her career Erna examined over 10,000 brain-wave recordings and displayed an uncanny talent for recognizing patterns and understanding their significance.

Marija Gimbutas (1921–1994)
Archaeologist, folklorist

Marija Gimbutas was born in Lithuania but moved to the United States in 1949. She began her career combining the disciplines of archaeology and mythology at Harvard University. In 1964 she went to the University of California at Los Angeles to teach European archaeology and Indo-European studies.

Gimbutas looked for women's place in eastern European prehistory. In the late 1960s and early 1970s, she conducted archaeological digs in Yugoslavia, Italy, and Greece. There she found evidence of societies where it seemed women had status equal to or greater than men. She uncovered prehistoric temples over 7,000 years old that contained statuettes of women preparing food. Many feminist scholars emphasize the importance of food preparation, traditionally a woman's activity, in the study of culture. It can be considered both a form of technology and a sacred act.

Traditionally anthropologists have described most societies as based on male authority. Gimbutas theorized that many prehistoric societies were led by women—also that ancient societies were cooperative and peaceful until men became more influential. She published 20 books, including *Gods and Goddesses of Old Europe, 7000–3500 B.C.* (1974) and *The Language of the Goddess* (1989).

Eleanor Touroff Glueck (1898–1972)
Criminologist

BORN IN BROOKLYN, ELEANOR TOUROFF MET THE lawyer Sheldon Glueck when she was a graduate student at the New School for Social Research in New York City. They married in 1922, and moved to Boston. There Eleanor attended the Harvard Graduate School of Education, where Dr. Richard Cabot, a physician with an interest in social work, was influential in shaping her research methods and focus. Eleanor worked with Sheldon to write *Five Hundred Criminal Careers* (1930), a study that followed former prisoners for five years after their parole.

The Gluecks worked together for over 40 years. Eleanor was a determined, painstaking researcher, especially good at separating fact from rumor. Between 1940 and 1950, they compared 500 socially adjusted boys with 500 boys in reform school, checking on them at intervals until they reached the age of 31. Using this information, they compiled the Gluecks' Social Prediction Tables to help predict criminal behavior in children. Some sociologists were concerned about how the tables might be used, but many found them valuable. Most would agree that Eleanor Glueck's work was instrumental in promoting the use of sustained research as a tool in social work.

Jane Goodall (1934–)
Primatologist, conservationist

ENGLISH-BORN JANE GOODALL WAS 23 YEARS OLD when she fulfilled her lifelong dream of visiting Africa. While there, she sought out Louis Leakey, a paleontologist who was researching at Olduvai Gorge in what is now Tanzania. Leakey hired Goodall as a secretary and encouraged her talents and enthusiasm. In spite of her lack of formal education, he suggested that she study the chimpanzees that lived on the shore of nearby Lake Tanganyika.

Goodall's research lasted six years. She began by observing from a clearing above the lake, so that the chimpanzees would not flee. Even though she knew chimpanzees have many of the same genes we do, she still was surprised at how much their behavior resembled that of humans. They held hands and greeted each other with hugs and kisses. She saw one

chimp use a stick to catch termites to eat. The ability to use tools was thought to belong to humans alone.

After nearly a year, Goodall left her observation post to establish a personal relationship with the chimpanzees. She withstood threatening displays from them for six months. Finally, they accepted her and even began to visit her camp when she left bananas for them.

Scientists were initially skeptical of Goodall's work. They thought her descriptions of behaviors indicated an overly emotional involvement in her study subjects. Gradually, though, she gained the respect of the scientific community. She has received many awards for her scientific work and conservation efforts on behalf of chimps and other wild animals. In 1977 she founded the Jane Goodall Institute, currently based in Washington, D.C., to continue her research.

Maria Emma Gray (1787–1876)
Conchologist, algologist

MARIA GRAY, A WIDOW WITH TWO CHILDREN, married one of her late husband's cousins in 1826. John Edward Gray was a scientist for the Natural History Department at the British Museum in London. The cultured Maria took an immediate interest in John's work. She made illustrations for him and used her own money to pay for journeys to gather samples and view other naturalists' collections.

Maria Gray became an expert in the study of mollusks, a group of soft-bodied animals that often have shells—snails, clams, and squid, for example. She arranged a collection at the British Museum and made thousands of illustrations, which were published in a five-volume work, *Figures of Molluscous Animals* (1842–1874).

Gray was an authority on the marine plants known as algae, too. She organized the collection at Kew Gardens, London's famous botanical gardens, in addition to the British Museum's collection. To help children learn about algae, she created special displays for use in schools. Her private collection of algae was donated to the Museum of the University of Cambridge after her death.

Alice Hamilton (1869–1970)
Physician, industrial toxicologist

D R. ALICE HAMILTON ALWAYS WANTED TO MAKE a real contribution to society. She got her M.D. from the University of Michigan in 1893 and spent a year studying in Germany. Returning to America in 1895, she moved into Hull House in Chicago. There she began a lifelong friendship with Jane Addams and met many women who shared her desire to improve the world. Although she was active at Hull House, Hamilton didn't find her true calling until she was 41, when she came across information about dangerous substances used in manufacturing.

At the time no laws in America protected industrial laborers from hazardous conditions in the workplace. Hamilton changed that. She began by studying lead poisoning in Illinois, eventually identifying 77 procedures that used lead and confirming 578 cases of poisoning. She researched "phossy jaw," a painful affliction of workers in match factories, who had to use phosphorus. She discovered that the mercury used to make felt hats was the cause of a strange behavior, known as "hatter's shakes." Her findings that picric acid, used to make explosives during World War II, could be fatal angered factory owners. They tried, unsuccessfully, to stop her investigations.

Hamilton's research and activism led to the creation of some of the first workers' compensation laws. She defined the field of industrial medicine and wrote its earliest texts, beginning with *Industrial Poisons in the United States* (1925). She was also active in the pacifist movement, although her concern about Nazism led her to support World War II. She lived long enough to voice her protest to the war in Vietnam.

Harriet Boyd Hawes (1871–1945)
Archaeologist

A LTHOUGH HARRIET HAWES WAS BORN IN BOSTON, raised in Greenfield, and went to Smith College, she was fascinated by the ancient cultures of lands far from Massachusetts. In 1896 she went to the American School of Classical Studies in Athens, Greece. Becoming interested in archaeology, she traveled to Crete, where she discovered tombs from the Iron Age, about 3,000 years ago. The thesis she wrote about them earned her a master's degree from Smith College in 1901. That same year, and in 1903 and 1904, she led archaeological digs on Crete.

Hawes was the first person to discover and thoroughly excavate a town built by the Minoans, an ancient Cretan civilization that existed from 3000 B.C.E. to 1100 B.C.E., during the Bronze Age. The Archaeological Institute of America sent her on a lecture tour in 1902 to describe this important find. In 1909 she published the book *Crete: The Forerunner of Greece* with her husband, Charles Henry Hawes, a British archaeologist.

For several years Hawes raised a family and volunteered for social causes. She returned to

Massachusetts to lecture at Wellesley College in 1920. In 1936 she retired, a respected and influential scholar. Artifacts from her excavations are in the collections of several American museums.

Herrad of Landsberg (approximately 1105–1195)
Physician, natural scientist

THE CONVENTS OF THE MIDDLE AGES WERE OFTEN places of learning for women. Herrad of Landsberg, like Hildegard of Bingen, was a nun who was also a physician and scientist. She was the abbess of the Hohenburg convent in Alsace, where she taught, wrote, and practiced medicine.

Between 1160 and 1190, Herrad compiled the *Hortus deliciarum* (Garden of delights), an encyclopedia that included information on religion, history, geography, astronomy, botany, and medicine. Important terms were included in both Latin and German, and it was used as a teaching text for the members of the convent. The book's 636 elaborate illustrations may also have been done by Herrad. The encyclopedia survived for over 500 years, but when Strasbourg was bombed in 1870, the library where it was kept burned down. Luckily, much of it had been copied down before then.

Leta Stetter Hollingworth (1886–1939)
Educational psychologist

DURING THE EARLY 1900S, MANY SCIENTISTS TRIED to prove that men were, by nature, intellectually superior to women. They also argued that the physical demands of childbearing and menstruation made women unfit for jobs perceived as "men's work." Leta Hollingworth challenged these notions.

A native of Nebraska, Hollingworth came to New York City as a newlywed. She intended to become a schoolteacher, but she discovered that married women weren't permitted to teach in the city's public schools. Instead, she went to graduate school for education and psychology at Columbia University. She researched sexual stereotyping, testing newborns of both sexes for physical and intellectual traits. She also tested college

men and women. Analyzing her data, she found no significant differences.

Hollingworth joined the staff at Teachers College in 1916. In the 1920s she began to study gifted children. She found that many children who had exceptionally high IQs felt isolated and lonely, while the children whose IQs were between 125 and 155 tended to be better adjusted. A year after her death, Teachers' College honored her with a conference on educating gifted learners.

Karen Danielsen Horney (1885–1952)
Psychiatrist, psychoanalyst

IN 1911, NEWLY GRADUATED FROM MEDICAL SCHOOL in Berlin, Karen Horney underwent psychoanalysis for a number of reasons. She had negative feelings about her overly strict father, who had opposed her getting an education. The birth of her first daughter created conflict between her role as a mother and her career. There was also trouble in her marriage.

Horney's experiences with analysis weren't always productive, but they helped shape her own

> "There are many things that belong to, or are prerequisites for, doing good analytic work. For instance, the whole question of understanding, of interpreting at the right time and in the right spirit, of having a feeling for dreams, and so on and so forth. But basic even to these prerequisites is a certain kind of attentiveness to the patient. I think there are three categories by which we can describe this quality. . . . [T]hese three categories of attentiveness are wholeheartedness, comprehensiveness, and productiveness."
>
> **KAREN HORNEY**
> *Final Lectures,* 1987

theories. She proposed altering Sigmund Freud's male-centered view so that women's psychological development could be viewed on its own terms, not in relation to men's. Horney's views were well received, and a former colleague offered her a job in Chicago. In 1932, partly because of her concern at the growing power of the Nazis, she left Germany. Two years later, she settled in New York City.

There she continued to move further away from Freud's theories by emphasizing the culture's effects on normal development. In 1939, with her book *New Ways in Psychoanalysis*, Horney challenged many of Freud's basic assertions. She questioned whether women truly felt incomplete and inferior in comparison to men, and suggested that their ability to bear children might even be something that men envied. The outraged members of the New York Psychoanalytic Society and Institute limited her associations with their group. So Horney and others formed the American Association for the Advancement of Psychoanalysis.

Karen Horney's theories changed the view of normal psychological development, especially as it applies to girls and women. Her work has affected most areas of modern psychiatry.

Vilma Hugonnai-Wartha (1847–1922)
Physician

VILMA HUGONNAI, THE DAUGHTER OF A COUNT, married György Szillassy in 1865. When their little girl died at the age of six, the grief-stricken Vilma decided to become a pediatric physician. She had chosen a difficult career for her time, but with determination, she became the first Hungarian woman recognized as an M.D.

Hugonnai studied medicine in Zurich, Switzerland. She passed her oral M.D. exam in 1879 but, as a woman, was only awarded a midwife's certificate. Moving back to Budapest, she became an assistant to the chemist Vince Wartha. Later, Vilma's first marriage having ended, the two married.

The Ministry of Culture finally accepted Hugonnai-Wartha's education as the equivalent of a medical degree in 1897. She began her practice, and her success paved the way for other improvements. After 1913 women doctors were given permission to practice in their own right, not just in association with men. By 1927 there were 273 female doctors in Hungary.

Harriot Kezia Hunt (1805–1875)
Physician

ALTHOUGH SHE NEVER ATTENDED MEDICAL SCHOOL, Harriot Hunt practiced medicine in the Boston area for over 30 years. She applied twice, unsuccessfully, to attend lectures at Harvard Medical School. Finally, she received an honorary Doctor of Medicine degree in 1853 from the Female Medical College of Philadelphia.

Hunt was inspired to go into medicine by the experiences of her sister, Sarah. In 1830 Sarah fell ill, but the harsh medications prescribed only seemed to make things worse. At last a medical couple named the Motts came to town, and their treatment worked. The sisters studied with them; then, with their mother's encouragement, opened their own practice in 1835. Although they couldn't work in hospitals, over time they became popular with women and those who had endured ineffective treatment. The sisters' common-sense philosophy of health was based on preventing disease through rest, good diet, exercise, and hygiene.

Marriage took Sarah away from the practice in 1840, but Harriot continued and broadened her work. She formed the Ladies' Physiological Society, leading informal talks about health. Her support of women's rights was a natural extension of her medical work. She felt that marriages should be partnerships and that women and men should be equals in society. In 1850 she attended the first national women's rights convention in Worcester, Massachusetts. She also campaigned to abolish slavery. Her autobiography, *Glances and Glimpses* (1856), tells the story of her life and era.

Kate Campbell Hurd-Mead (1867–1941)
Physician, medical historian

KATE HURD WANTED SO MUCH TO BECOME A doctor that she broke off an early engagement when her fiancé opposed her plans. Moving from Newburyport, Massachusetts, to Philadelphia, she entered the Woman's Medical College of Pennsylvania and graduated in 1888.

She soon made her home in Baltimore, Maryland. There she started a private practice and became the medical director at the Bryn Mawr

Her interests lay in the circulatory, respiratory, and nervous systems of animals. After conducting successful zoological experiments at Bryn Mawr College, she was invited by a professor at the University of Strassburg to study in Germany. However, Hyde's request to begin doctoral studies in Strassburg was rejected based on her sex. She transferred to Heidelberg University. Although one eminent professor, the physiologist Wilhelm Kühne, refused to work with her because she was a woman, other faculty supported her. In 1896 she became the first woman to graduate from Heidelberg University with a Ph.D.

Dr. Hyde wanted other women to have an easier time getting a scientific education. After studying at the Zoological Station in Naples, she set up a program for women there. She established scholarships at the University of Kansas, where she taught for over 20 years, at Cornell, and with the American Association of University Women.

School for Girls. With a colleague, Dr. Alice Hill, she established the Evening Dispensary for Working Women and Girls in Baltimore City. It provided health services for women and children and was a place where women doctors could practice.

After her marriage to an English professor, William Mead, she moved to Connecticut and helped to incorporate the Middlesex County Hospital. In 1925 Hurd-Mead retired from her practice and began researching the history of women in medicine. Information she collected in Europe, Asia, and Africa led to the publication of two books, *Medical Women of America* (1933) and *A History of Women in Medicine from the Earliest Times to the Beginning of the Nineteenth Century* (1938). She died of a heart attack after trying to save a man who had lost consciousness while fighting a fire on her property.

Ida Henrietta Hyde (1857–1945)
Physiologist, educator

Although Ida Hyde had to begin working at age 16, she was determined to educate herself. She studied in her spare time, and started college at the University of Chicago when she was 24, but ran out of money after a year. It would be seven years before she could afford to enroll at Cornell University; she graduated in 1891.

Libbie Henrietta Hyman (1888–1969)
Zoologist

Libbie Hyman managed to escape her difficult childhood and become an expert in zoology. She grew up in Fort Dodge, Iowa, in a poor immigrant family. Her parents argued often, and her mother was especially difficult to get along with. Libbie reacted to her situation by focusing on school and learning about the plant life in her neighborhood.

In 1906 a scholarship from the University of Chicago saved her from a dismal job in a factory, gluing labels on boxes. She stayed at the university, earning a Ph.D. in zoology in 1915 and working as a lab assistant until 1931. Meanwhile, she wrote two successful laboratory manuals. The resulting income allowed her to travel abroad, then move to New York City and concentrate on an ambitious writing project. Hyman's masterpiece, *The Invertebrates* (1940–1967), is a six-volume

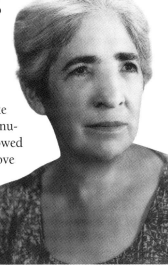

study of animals that do not have skeletons, such as worms. In 1937 the American Museum of Natural History offered her a work space, and she made use of this office until the end of her life. Hyman had planned to add another two volumes to *The Invertebrates*, but Parkinson's disease limited her research in her later years.

Elsie Maud Inglis (1864–1917)
Surgeon, physician

AFTER A CHILDHOOD SPENT IN INDIA, WHERE HER father worked for the British East India Company, Elsie Inglis returned with her family to their native Scotland. She earned her medical degree in 1892, after studying at Sophia Jex-Blake's Edinburgh School of Medicine and at schools in Glasgow and Dublin.

A skilled surgeon who was beloved by her patients, Inglis worked at the New Hospital for Women, founded by Elizabeth Garrett Anderson, and at the Edinburgh Bruntsfield Hospital. She also established her own practice. To promote women's medical careers, she established a maternity hospital that was managed and staffed by women. She also joined the suffrage movement, founding the Scottish Women's Suffrage Federation in 1906.

When World War I began in 1914, she arranged for women doctors to be sent to treat wounded soldiers. Although Britain refused their aid, the French and Belgian Red Cross welcomed their presence in France and Serbia. Inglis spent most of the war with the Serbian troops, continuing her job even after her hospital was captured, and patients and staff were made prisoners. By 1917 she was very ill, but she refused to evacuate unless her Serbian patients could be saved, too. At last, extremely weak, she returned to England on November 25th, but she died the following day.

Susan Isaacs (1885–1948)
Child psychologist

SUSAN ISAACS'S FATHER, A DEVOUT METHODIST, took her out of school when she was 15 because she said she had decided God didn't exist. Nevertheless, she went on to graduate from

Manchester University in 1912, thoroughly impressing her instructors there.

Her work at the experimental Malting House School in Cambridge provided material for many of her 14 books. The children there were encouraged to make their own decisions. Later, as head of the Department of Child Development at the University of London Institute of Education, she made even more progress. Arriving in 1933, she created a world-class center of child development out of what had been an understaffed and undistinguished department.

Her theories about childhood development were aligned with those of Melanie Klein. She emphasized their need for freedom and spontaneity, but felt structure and routine were also essential. Her last two books, *The Family in a World at War* (1942) and *Troubles of Children and Parents* (1948), focused on children's experiences during war and divorce.

Mary Putnam Jacobi (1842–1906)
Physician

THE FIRST WOMAN ACCEPTED AT THE ÉCOLE DE Médecine in France was an American, Mary Putnam. The faculty did not want her there, but she persuaded the minister of education to admit her anyway. Actually, Putnam had already received an M.D. from the Female Medical College of Pennsylvania in 1864. She went to France because

she was frustrated with the quality of her medical education. After graduating with honors in 1871, she left Paris and returned home, determined to improve women's educational opportunities there.

Putnam worked as a teacher, physician, and activist. At Dr. Elizabeth Blackwell's medical college, she was considered a challenging instructor. In addition to operating a private practice, she worked at many New York hospitals to establish medical services for children. She created the Association for the Advancement of the Medical Education of Women and was its president from 1874 to 1903. During the 1890s, she also worked for the woman suffrage movement. She published over 100 articles, mostly on medical topics but also about suffrage and education.

After breaking two other engagements, she married Dr. Abraham Jacobi in 1873. He is considered the founder of children's medicine in the United States. Sadly, two of their three children died young. Still, they had a happy marriage, doing much of their work together, and sharing a concern for social change.

Mae Jemison (1956–)
Physician, astronaut

MAE JEMISON HAS NOT ONLY TRAVELED ALL OVER the world, she has traveled *out* of the world. On September 12, 1992, she became the first black woman in space. She and six other astronauts spent eight days on the shuttle *Endeavour*. Her experiments focused on the effect of weightlessness on calcium in the bones and on tissue growth. She also investigated the possibility of using biofeedback to control motion sickness, an experiment that aroused the interest of astronauts and space agencies worldwide.

Although Jemison always knew she wanted to be an astronaut, she began her career as a physician. She entered college when she was only 16 and, following graduation, went to New York City to attend the Cornell University Medical College. She studied and worked in Cuba, Kenya, and Thailand, and spent two and a half years in West Africa with the Peace Corps. Her application to NASA to become an astronaut-in-training was accepted in 1987.

In addition to her career in science, Dr. Jemison has always pursued many interests. As an undergraduate at Stanford University, she majored in both chemical engineering and African American studies.

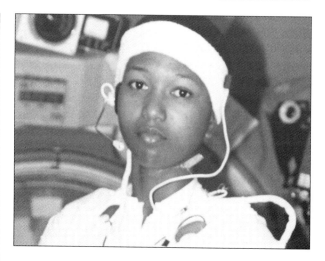

She also participated in sports, dance, and theater projects and was the first woman to be elected president of the Black Student Union at Stanford. She is passionate about women's rights and identifies herself as a "womanist." The year after her spaceflight, Jemison combined her skills as a doctor and astronaut and founded the Jemison Group, a research and development company.

Sophia Jex-Blake (1840–1912)
Physician

SOPHIA JEX-BLAKE WAS AN OPINIONATED WOMAN whose forceful style contrasted with that of her more diplomatic ally, Elizabeth Garrett Anderson, and often created disagreements between them.

"If a child falls down-stairs, and is more or less seriously hurt, is it the father or the mother (where both are without medical training) who is most equal to the emergency, and who applies the needful remedies in the first instance? . . . Of course it may be said that such practice is by no means scientific, but merely empirical, and this I readily allow; but that fact in no way affects my argument that women are *naturally* inclined and fitted for medical practice."

SOPHIA JEX-BLAKE
Medical Women: A Thesis and a History, 1886

However, her persistence played a key role in open-ing the English medical world to women.

American women had begun to earn medical degrees in 1865, so Jex-Blake went there to study under Drs. Lucy Sewall and Elizabeth Blackwell. After her father's death forced her to return to England, she applied to the University of London, only to be rejected because the school's charter specifically excluded women. After an initial rejection from Edinburgh University, she and four friends were allowed to begin special "women only" classes. But the battle had barely begun. They were still forbidden to take the final qualifying exam for a degree. During their time there, one of the women was denied a prize she had earned, and their presence caused a riot. Their plight became a national issue, and the women gained public support. Jex-Blake founded the London School of Medicine for Women in 1874, even though students would not yet be able to obtain degrees.

Finally, in 1876, the British government passed a bill allowing universities to grant M.D.s to women. Sophia Jex-Blake received her degree from Queens University in Dublin the following year. She estab-lished a successful practice in Edinburgh, where, in 1886, she founded the Edinburgh School of Medicine for Women.

newspaper column, as well as many scientific arti-cles. Highly regarded by her peers, she was the first woman to be elected president of the American Gastroenterological Association in 1942.

Sara Murray Jordan (1884–1959)
Physician

Sara Jordan already had a Ph.D. in classical literature when, at the age of 33, she decided to become a doctor. Tufts Medical School in Medford, Massachusetts, accepted her, but she had to make up the undergraduate chemistry and zoology courses she had never taken while studying the classics. In 1921 she graduated at the top of her class.

Jordan opened her own practice, and at the same time, was one of the founding members of the influ-ential Lahey Clinic in Boston. Her specialty was gas-troenterology, treating diseases of the stomach and intestines. She was a popular doctor, who combined a practical medical approach with a witty manner.

One of Dr. Jordan's patients was Harold W. Ross, the editor of the *New Yorker* magazine. He encour-aged her to publish her advice about ulcers and diet for the public. The result was a cookbook, *Good Food for Bad Stomachs* (1951). Later she wrote a syndicated

Anandibai Joshee (1865–1887)
Physician

Anandibai Joshee's life was short, but she helped bring about revolutionary changes in the health care available to Indian women. Unlike most girls in India, she received an education, because her father and her husband both encouraged her to study. Joshee resolved to become a doctor when her daughter died ten days after being born.

Many people were opposed to Joshee's plans to travel alone to the United States to attend medical school. So in 1883 she defended herself eloquently to a group at Serampore College in Calcutta—in per-haps the first public speech by an Indian woman. Eight months later she boarded a steamship bound for America.

Joshee graduated from the Woman's Medical College of Pennsylvania in 1886 and returned to India to head the female ward at Albert Edward Hospital in Kolhapur. She died less than a year later from tuberculosis she had contracted in America. Still, she had impressed many people, and other women began to follow her example.

Elizabeth Kenny (1886–1952)
Physical therapist

POLIO WAS A DREADED AFFLICTION FOR MANY YEARS. The disease, caused by a virus, is extremely painful, usually strikes children, and often cripples or kills. In 1955 Dr. Jonas Salk introduced a vaccination that banished polio epidemics, at least from developed countries. But before that, Elizabeth Kenny's treatment eased the suffering of many polio patients.

Kenny, a native of New South Wales, Australia, trained as a nurse. She was 23 when she encountered her first case of polio in a two-year-old girl. Unaware that doctors usually kept the patient's limbs immobile for weeks, she applied hot, moist rags instead. The child soon felt better. Kenny went on to develop a program that included the hot rags, passive exercises, and therapy to teach afflicted muscles how to move again.

The "Kenny treatment" was surprisingly controversial, even though she reported an astounding 80-percent success rate at preventing paralysis. Australian doctors were so opposed to her method that, for a time, it was condemned by the Royal Commission. Even so, Kenny opened clinics in Australia, England, and the United States. In 1941 the National Infantile Paralysis Foundation, an American organization, endorsed her ideas, and soon after, the Kenny Institute was established in Minneapolis, Minnesota. "Sister" Kenny received many honors, including an invitation to the White House to meet President Franklin Roosevelt, a polio survivor.

"... historians are concerned primarily with written records, and the earliest systems of writing were only invented some five thousand years ago, whereas man was evolved from his ape-like ancestors about half-a-million years ago. In the study of man during this immensely long period, archaeology is necessary, for archaeology deals with all the material remains of man, the objects he used and made, his dwelling places and defensive structures, his tools and weapons, the remains of his food, his own bones and burial places, and, from these, deduces how he lived."

KATHLEEN KENYON
Beginning in Archaeology, 1952

Kathleen Mary Kenyon (1906–1978)
Archaeologist

KATHLEEN KENYON GREW UP AROUND ANCIENT objects. Her father, Sir Frederick Kenyon, was a director of London's British Museum, and Kathleen made a career of going to the source of those treasures. Kenyon participated in her first dig in 1929, when she went with Dr. Gertrude Caton-Thompson's crew to Zimbabwe. She learned many of her techniques while working with Sir Mortimer Wheeler, whose scientific methods were widely celebrated.

Kenyon made her most dramatic discoveries at the Mound of Jericho during the 1950s. Jericho figures prominently in the Bible as a city seized after the Israelite general Joshua sounds his army's trumpets, causing the walls to tumble. Kenyon found evidence that the walls had fallen at about the right time—around 1400 B.C.E.—but probably because of an earthquake. She also discovered that the site was settled over 9,000 years ago and that agriculture started there around 7000 B.C.E. Kenyon went on to conduct other important digs in Jerusalem.

An educator as well as a field worker, Kenyon was acting director of the London Institute of Archaeology during World War II and director of the British School of Archaeology in Jerusalem from 1951 to 1966. Her books include *Digging Up Jericho* (1957) and *Digging Up Jerusalem* (1974). In 1973, in recognition of her role in uncovering the biblical Middle East, she was made a Dame of the British Empire.

Kil Chung-Hee (1899–1990)
Physician

I T WAS UNUSUAL FOR KOREAN GIRLS TO RECEIVE AN education during the early 1900s, but Kil Chung-Hee's grandfather encouraged her to go to school. Traveling to Japan, she attended the Tokyo Women's Medical College and graduated in 1923.

In 1925 she married Dr. Kim Tak-Won, and they eventually had three children. Dr. Kil began working in Seoul at the Dong-Dae-Moon Women's hospital, directed by an American woman, Dr. Rosetta Hall. Soon Kil realized how much women practitioners were needed in Korea; many women refused to see male doctors. To address this issue, she joined with her husband and Hall to found the Chosen Women's Medical Training Institute.

The Institute faced several difficulties, including the prejudice of many male physicians. The Japanese, who ruled Korea from 1910 to 1945, opposed the Institute's development and took charge of it in 1938. Kil operated a private practice and taught at Ewha Women's University until her retirement in 1964. By then her contributions to medicine had begun to be recognized.

Helen Dean King (1869–1955)
Biologist

T HE EDITORS OF THE 1906 EDITION OF *AMERICAN Men of Science* put a star next to their entry about Dr. Helen Dean King—this meant that she was considered one of the country's top 1,000 scientists. Even the general public took an interest in her research, but they were shocked by it.

King worked at the Wistar Institute of Anatomy and Biology in Philadelphia for 42 years, and her famous research was with rats. Between 1909 and 1918, she bred 25 generations of rats, using mostly siblings, and compared the offspring with other rats. She concluded that inbreeding had not created a weaker strain. The newspapers sensationalized her findings, saying that King thought incest was acceptable.

King went on to study the domestication of rats. Starting with wild Norway rats, she catalogued a variety of traits and created strains in which specific characteristics could be studied. One of those has

become a standard for laboratory use. Again she made the news; this time reporters marveled at the sight of a woman handling rats.

King published numerous scientific papers. She was also a professor of embryology, a member of the institute's advisory board, and associate editor of the *Journal of Morphology and Physiology*. She didn't retire until she was 80 years old.

Melanie Klein (1882–1960)
Psychoanalyst

B ORN IN VIENNA, AUSTRIA, MELANIE REIZES wanted to go to medical school but gave up her studies when she married Arthur Stephan Klein in 1903. They had three children, but it was a troubled marriage. Suffering from depression, Melanie read Sigmund Freud's *On Dreams* (1901) and was inspired. In 1914, while in Budapest, Hungary, she began treatment with Sandor Ferenczi, a colleague of Freud's. He encouraged her to study the application of analysis to children.

In 1921 Klein became the child therapist at the Berlin Psychoanalytic Institute, where she developed her most influential ideas. Giving a young patient toys that represented family members, she observed the child's play and concluded that meaningful subconscious feelings were being expressed through his actions. Her idea of "play therapy" is still widely used in treating young children. As Klein explained in her book, *The Psychoanalysis of Children* (1932), she believed that childhood neurosis developed during the very first months of life. For several years support among analysts was split between Klein and Anna Freud, another major psychoanalyst of the day, who disagreed with Klein's concept. Over time, though, both women's ideas have proved influential in the field.

Klein moved to London in 1926 and spent the rest of her life there. In the 1950s she moved away from her work with children, concentrating instead on treating adults, writing, and teaching.

Mathilde Krim (1926–)
Virologist, geneticist

COMPASSION FOR OTHERS HAS ALWAYS BEEN A force in Mathilde Krim's life. Growing up in Switzerland, she knew her parents were anti-Semitic, but didn't think much about it. Then, after World War II, she was horrified to learn about Nazi concentration camps. She immediately joined a Zionist group, eventually converting to Judaism and moving to Rehovot, Israel. Since she had trained in biology at the University of Geneva, she became a cancer researcher at the Weizmann Institute of Science there.

In 1958 she married the businessman Arthur B. Krim and moved to New York. Through her examination of the role of viruses in cancer at the Sloan-Kettering Center for Cancer Research, she became aware of interferon, a naturally occurring virus inhibitor. It took a great deal of research, and she had to overcome much scientific disagreement, but eventually she helped prove that interferon could be used to combat a rare kind of leukemia.

Since the 1980s, Krim's work has centered on AIDS. She was one of the first people to realize the devastation it would cause. Her focus has been on public education, both to explain how to prevent the disease and to discourage discrimination against AIDS sufferers. She established several research and funding organizations, including the American Foundation for AIDS Research, or AMFAR. Her scientific expertise and her ability to attract public figures to support the cause has made her a key figure in the fight against AIDS.

Elisabeth Kübler-Ross (1926–)
Psychiatrist, thanatologist

IN 1965 THE SWISS-BORN DR. ELISABETH Kübler-Ross was a psychiatrist on staff at the University of Chicago Medical School and had already done some work with the terminally ill. A group of students from the Chicago Theological Seminary asked her to advise them on a project about death. She helped them coordinate conversations with terminally ill patients, who proved eager to participate.

Kübler-Ross determined that there were five stages people experience when they are dying: denial, anger, bargaining, depression, and finally, acceptance. Not every patient goes through every phase in order, but most experience some of them. The emotions are also common among people confronting other crises, such as divorce. Her resulting book, *On Death and Dying* (1969), did much to change the way terminally ill patients are treated.

In 1968 Kübler-Ross met a patient who had revived after being declared dead, and she began investigating life after death. This work is much more controversial. Doctors have criticized her for being unscientific and for contradicting her earlier work, which helped people accept death. Still, she has remained a respected authority on thanatology, the study of death. A stroke forced Kübler-Ross to retire in 1995. She then published *The Wheel of Life: A Memoir of Living and Dying* (1997).

Mary Leakey (1913–1996)
Archaeologist

THE ENGLISH-BORN MARY LEAKEY'S INTEREST IN archaeology began when she was a girl accompanying her artist father on visits to prehistoric caves in southwestern France. Later, a chance meeting with the archaeologist Dorothy Liddell convinced her that it was a reasonable career for a woman. She assisted Liddell in the field from 1930 to 1934, and began publishing illustrations of the finds. In 1933 she met Louis B. Leakey. After the two were married in 1936, they worked as a team.

Mary made many discoveries on her own. In 1948 in Kenya, she found 30 pieces of a *Proconsul africanus* skull of the Miocene period (about 20 million years ago). This evidence of a direct ancestor of humans supported the theory that human life began in Africa. At Olduvai Gorge in 1959, she found a second skull, *Zinjanthropus*, which was briefly thought to be the "missing link" between ape and man.

One of Leakey's favorite projects made use of her artistic skills. In 1951 she traced and transferred to paper 1,600 Stone Age paintings from caves in Tanzania. The paintings, filled with details about clothes, hair, and musical instruments, provided information that couldn't have been discovered through bone and tool artifacts. She was equally enthusiastic about her 1978 discovery in Tanzania of the 3.5-million-year-old footprints of two adults and a child.

Louis and Mary Leakey

After Louis died in 1972, Mary began speaking in public, a task he had done for them in the past. Her lectures were popular with scientists and the general public. She received many awards, including the National Geographic Society's Hubbard Medal and the Bradford Washburn Award.

Rita Levi-Montalcini (1909–)
Neurobiologist

RITA LEVI-MONTALCINI, BORN IN ITALY, KNEW THAT she didn't want to take on the traditional role of housewife and mother. When her former governess died of cancer, she decided to become a doctor. She entered the Turin School of Medicine in 1930, where Dr. Giuseppe Levi became her mentor. She began studying nervous system cells, her area of research for the rest of her career. During World War II, she had to leave her job because she was Jewish. She turned her bedroom into a lab where she could study the nervous system of chicken embryos.

In 1947 she accepted the invitation of Dr. Viktor Hamburger to come to Washington University in St. Louis, Missouri. Her job there, intended to last six months, extended to 30 years. Still using chicken embryos, Levi-Montalcini observed that cancerous tumors from mice caused the formation of nerve cells in chickens. She hypothesized that a hormone-like chemical was responsible for this. Working with Dr. Stanley Cohen, she identified the chemical, which they called Nerve Growth Factor (NGF). In 1986 they were awarded the Nobel Prize in medicine or physiology for their work.

After 1961 Levi-Montalcini began spending part of each year in Italy with her twin sister. In 1987 President Ronald Reagan awarded her the National Medal of Science. Her research has been useful in studies of Alzheimer's disease, cancer, and birth defects.

Lin Ch'iao-chih (1901–1983)
Physician

LIN CH'IAO-CHIH, OR MOTHER LIN, FELT THAT HER country had suffered through many difficulties, and the Chinese people deserved a doctor with "conscience." She earned her degree from Peking

Union Medical College in 1929 and studied in England and America, as well.

In 1942 Lin established the Department of Obstetrics and Gynecology at the Zhonghe Hospital in Peking. Among her many humanitarian activities was her involvement with the Barefoot Doctors movement, a program to teach people in rural areas basic first aid and health care. By 1968 over 29,000 people had been trained.

Lin continued her career, and meanwhile dramatic political changes took place in China. The Japanese occupied the country during World War II, and not long after that the Communists took control. She was so beloved that Chairman Mao invited her to attend a state ceremony in 1949. Lin was too busy even to respond. It became an affectionate joke among the people that she had dared to say "no" to the Chairman.

Lilian Murray Lindsay (1871–1959)
Dentist

LONDON-BORN LILIAN MURRAY WANTED TO become a dentist, but women students were not allowed at England's National Dental Hospital. However, the dean of that school told her she would be allowed to study in Scotland and suggested that she apply there. In 1895 Murray graduated from the Edinburgh Dental Hospital and became the first British woman licensed to practice dentistry. Ten years later she married a former teacher from the school, Robert Lindsay. They shared a dental practice in Edinburgh and then moved to London.

The British Dental Association benefited greatly from Lilian Lindsay's almost 40-year-long association with them. She became their librarian in 1920 and gathered an impressive collection of books. In 1933 she was elected president of the metropolitan branch, and in 1946 she became the first woman president of the entire association.

An avid historian, she published *A Short History of Dentistry* in 1933 and led the historical section of the Royal Society of Medicine from 1850 to 1852. One of the greatest of her many awards came in 1958, when the British Dental Association granted her special honorary member status.

Clemence Sophia Lozier (1813–1888)
Physician, social reformer

CLEMENCE LOZIER MARRIED YOUNG, AND, AFTER her husband, Abraham, became an invalid, she started a girl's school in her home to support the family. Among the subjects she taught her students were female anatomy and physiology, very unusual information to provide to girls at that time.

After studying with her physician brother for several years, she attended Syracuse Medical College and graduated in 1853. She opened a practice in New York City specializing in obstetrics and gynecology. Her popularity as a physician opened her eyes to women's need to have information about their bodies. She began giving lectures, and opened a medical library for her patients.

With the help of Elizabeth Cady Stanton, she founded the New York Medical College and Hospital for Women in 1863. Lozier served as dean and a professor at the college for almost 25 years. Dr. Elizabeth Blackwell also founded a medical school for women, in 1868. However, the two doctors had different scientific philosophies. Blackwell did not consider Lozier's focus on homeopathic medicine legitimate.

Lozier was extremely active in human rights. She opposed slavery and supported the temperance movement, prison reform, and Native American rights, among other issues. She was president of the New York Woman Suffrage Society and the National Woman Suffrage Association. Her death was mourned by the graduates of her school—who numbered more than 200 by 1888—as well as women's rights activists.

Wangari Muta Maathai (1940–)
Biologist, environmentalist

IN RURAL KENYA THERE IS A LINK BETWEEN TOO little firewood and malnutrition. When women have to search too long for wood, they have less time to prepare meals and feed their children. This is why Dr. Wangari Maathai founded the Green Belt Movement in 1977, hiring local women to cultivate tree seedlings and distribute them for planting. The program has additional benefits, including slowing the deforestation of the countryside.

In 1989 Maathai campaigned to prevent construction of a huge complex in Uhuru Park, the largest public green space in Nairobi. The Kenyan government resented her opposition, but the battle was successful; investors were convinced to withdraw their funding. Unfortunately, since then Maathai has suffered government persecution for her political activism.

Maathai received much of her education in America. She graduated from Mount St. Scholastica College in Kansas in 1964 and earned her master's in biology at the University of Pittsburgh. Returning home, she became the first woman to get a Ph.D. from the University of Nairobi. The recipient of many honors, she was one of 25 women celebrated by the United Nations Environmental Programme in 1997.

Barbara McClintock (1902–1992)
Geneticist

BARBARA MCCLINTOCK LEARNED SHE HAD WON the Nobel Prize for 1983 when she heard the announcement on the radio—she didn't have a phone. She received the honor for her research on genes and chromosomes, the material inside cells that contains information about inherited characteristics. The accepted theory at the time was that genes were arranged on chromosomes in fixed, unchangeable lines. But McClintock found that genes could move from one chromosome to another, and that their movement was responsible for alterations in genetic traits.

McClintock first announced her theories in 1951 at the Cold Spring Harbor Symposium for Quantitative Biology. The description of her ten years of observation of kernel color patterns in Indian corn attracted little interest, though. In fact, in two decades of research, only three people asked to read her written work. But McClintock was never discouraged by others. She worked alone in her lab and had confidence in her theories.

Technology finally caught up with McClintock's research in the 1970s, when "jumping genes" were isolated in bacteria. Still, many did not believe her theories applied to plant and animal cells. It was not until she won the Nobel Prize in medicine or physiology that other scientists began looking seriously at her results. Mostly, it was her work—not the recognition for it—that McClintock loved. She continued working at Cold Spring Harbor, New York, until she was 90 years old.

Sidnie Milana Manton (1902–1979)
Zoologist

SIDNIE MANTON WAS BORN IN LONDON AND attended Girton College at Cambridge. She became an expert in the study of arthropods, a group of animals that includes spiders, crabs, barnacles, and giant water bugs. In the course of her research, she analyzed the movement of millipedes and centipedes and investigated the relationships between arthropods and other animal groups.

In 1929 Manton made an expedition to the Great Barrier Reef in Australia to study crustaceans, a class of arthropods that are identified by their two pairs of antennae and that usually live in the ocean. Later Manton returned to Girton and taught natural science from 1935 to 1942. During that time she married John Harding, who worked in the zoology department of the British Museum. She became a fellow of Britain's Royal Society in 1948 and received the Linnaean Gold Medal in 1963. Among her books is *Arthropods*, published in 1977.

Anna Morandi Manzolini (1716–1774)
Anatomist

MEDICAL STUDENTS NEED TO LEARN THE ANATOMY of the human body, but before refrigeration it was difficult to preserve human cadavers so they could be studied. During the 18th century, wax models were used instead.

Anna Manzolini first learned model-making from her husband, Giovanni, an anatomy professor at the university in Bologna, Italy. Her work helped to support their six children. She eventually became such an expert in anatomy that she could teach her husband's classes when he became sick. When he died, she received a job at the university and, by 1760, was a full-fledged professor.

Manzolini's intricately crafted, extremely accurate models received international recognition. She was elected to the Russian Royal Scientific Association as well as the British Royal Society. The university in Milan offered her a job, but she preferred to stay in Bologna. She made many discoveries about the human body through dissection, most notably the structure of eye muscles. Her personal collection of wax models became a valuable possession of the Medical Institute of Bologna.

Lillien Jane Martin (1851–1943)
Psychologist

LILLIEN MARTIN STARTED OUT AS A HIGH SCHOOL science teacher. By the time she was 43 years old, she had become head of the science department and vice-principal at Girls' High School in San Francisco. For most people this would have been an entire career, but Martin decided to make significant changes. She went to Germany to study at the University of Göttingen, earning a Ph.D. in psychology.

In 1899, at the age of 48, she was again in California, as a psychology professor at Stanford University. She also became involved with the women's rights movement and, in 1911, was elected vice-president of the northern California branch of the National College Equal Suffrage League. The year before her mandatory retirement at age 65, she became the first woman department head at Stanford.

Retirement didn't mean relaxation for Dr. Martin. Once more, she embarked on a new career. As a respected practicing psychologist, she opened clinics that specialized in counseling for preschoolers and the elderly. At the same time, she sought adventures, traveling alone to Russia and South America. At the age of 81 she decided to learn to drive—the automobile had been a newfangled invention when she was young, but by then it was commonplace. Then she took to the roads and made a solo excursion across the United States.

Margaret Mead (1901–1978)
Anthropologist

MARGARET MEAD ADVANCED THE METHODS OF anthropology for scientists while fascinating the general public. She felt that behavior and character were shaped not only by biology, but by culture and social expectations. Often Mead studied other cultures to provide a way to look at her own. In her first book, *Coming of Age in Samoa* (1928), she documented the experience of adolescence in the Samoan Islands and contrasted it with adolescence in western cultures. She concluded that the turmoil experienced by teenagers in western society was caused by culture and not by biology. The book,

like many of her publications, was very popular and exposed the public to the field of anthropology.

Many influences attracted Mead to study anthropology. Her parents, Edward and Emily Fogg Mead of Philadelphia, were progressive in their views of racial equality, women's rights, and education. She was educated at home by her grandmother, a teacher, for several years. Because of her family's support and outlook, she never doubted that she would have a successful career. As a graduate student at Columbia University in New York, she studied under Franz Boas and his teaching assistant, Ruth Benedict.

Mead spent time in New Guinea and Bali as well as Samoa. In addition to her field research and writing, she was curator at the American Museum of Natural History, a professor at Columbia University, and a popular public speaker. Her works include *Male and Female: A Study of the Sexes in a Changing World* (1949), *Culture and Commitment* (1970), and her autobiography, *Blackberry Winter* (1972).

Dorothy Reed Mendenhall (1874–1964)
Physician

I N 1907 DR. DOROTHY MENDENHALL'S FIRST CHILD, a daughter, died when she was just a few hours old. This experience, which also left Mendenhall with

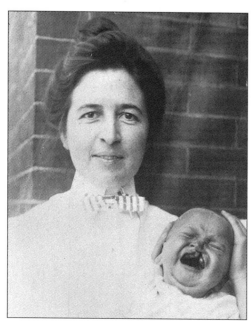

injuries and illness, steered her toward the study of infant mortality in the United States. She was already a noted medical researcher. Six years earlier, as a student at Johns Hopkins Medical School in Baltimore, she had received international attention for her work on Hodgkin's Disease, thought to be a form of tuberculosis. Mendenhall disproved that theory by discovering that a certain kind of blood cell was always present in sufferers.

Mendenhall, who worked at the University of Wisconsin, opened the state's first infant health clinic in Madison in 1915. By 1937 Madison had the lowest infant mortality rate in the country. After 1917, she also served as a medical officer for the United States Children's Bureau and made her influence felt across the nation.

Discovering that childhood malnutrition was common in America, Mendenhall instituted programs to weigh and measure children and established a standard for assessing their health. In 1926 she began a study that compared childbirth practices in the United States to those used in Denmark, where midwives were common and mortality rates were lower. She concluded that Danish midwives interfered less in the natural process of birth and therefore caused fewer unnecessary complications. She recommended that similar practices be adopted in America.

Maria Sibylla Merian (1647–1717)
Entomologist, scientific illustrator

M ARIA MERIAN CAME TO THE WORLD OF SCIENCE through art. Seventeenth-century Europeans were crazy about flowers; everyone wanted flower paintings, flower engravings, and flowers embroidered on fabric. Maria, born in Frankfurt, Germany, was the daughter of a famous botanical engraver, Matthäus Merian, who died when she was young. She learned painting from her stepfather, Jacob Marrel. In 1665 she married one of Marrel's students, Johann Andreas Graff. They had two daughters but eventually divorced.

By 1669 Merian had begun studying and drawing insects. Over several years she published a three-volume work, *The Wonderful Transformation of Caterpillars and Their Singular Plant Nourishment* (1679–1717), which contained drawings of 186 insects in different developmental stages. She was the first entomologist to collect caterpillar eggs so

Naming the Plants and Animals

Not long after Maria Merian died, scientists —starting with the Swedish botanist Carolus Linnaeus—began to create a uniform system, or taxonomy, for naming living things. Merian's numerous publications were widely consulted in this process. Linnaeus grouped organisms by characteristics, giving them two-part Latin names. The first name, always capitalized, identifies the genus of the animal or plant, and the second identifies the species. Organisms that belong to the same genus are related, but usually only those of the same species breed and produce offspring. Peaches (*Prunus persica*) and sweet cherries (*Prunus avium*) belong to the same genus but different species. According to the Linnaean system, humans are designated as *Homo sapiens*.

that she could observe and draw the living creatures as they metamorphosed into butterflies and moths.

Merian and her daughter, Johanna, traveled to Suriname to conduct an extended study of South American insects in 1699. Although ill health forced them to return home two years later, Merian made many important drawings there. She spent the last years of her life in Amsterdam.

Ynes Enriquetta Julietta Mexia (1870–1938)
Botanist, explorer

YNES MEXIA'S EARLY LIFE WAS NOT A HAPPY ONE. She was born in Georgetown, D.C., to a Mexican official and his American wife. Her parents soon divorced, and she grew up in several different places. Her first husband died, and a second marriage was disastrous but short. In 1908 Mexia settled in San Francisco. When she was in her fifties, she became interested in botany.

In 1926, after she returned from a successful plant-collecting trip to Mexico, Mexia resolved to finance her future explorations by selling the plants she collected to universities and museums. One of her most daring exploits was the journey across South America that she began in 1929. Traveling by steamer for 25,000 miles (40,230 km) along the Amazon River, she trekked into the rain forest and collected plants whenever the ship stopped. The steamer route ended in Iquitos, Peru, so Mexia hired three local guides and went 5,000 miles (8,045 km) farther. She brought back 65,000 painstakingly prepared specimens.

Mexia collected plants in Mount McKinley Park in Alaska, and she made many trips to Central and South America. During one visit to Mexico, she collected 33,000 specimens, one of which, *Mexianthus mexicanus*, was named for her. Mexia worked for 13 adventurous years before dying of lung cancer, and she provided botanists with much important material to study.

Lillie Rosa Minoka-Hill (1876–1952)
Physician

LILLIE ROSA MINOKA WAS FIVE YEARS OLD WHEN her mother died and she left the Mohawk Indian reservation in New York. She was going to Philadelphia to live with her father, a Quaker physician. When she got older, she also decided to become a doctor. After graduating from the Women's Medical College in 1899, she cared for immigrant women and opened a private practice.

In 1905 she married Charles Hill, an Oneida Indian. They moved to his farm on the Oneida reservation in Wisconsin and lived in a small house with no running water. In the next nine years, Minoka-Hill gave birth to six children.

She began sharing information about remedies with the healers on the reservation. Soon she was treating patients again and decided to stay even after her husband died in 1916. She didn't have a Wisconsin medical license, so she couldn't charge for her services. Instead patients gave her food or worked on her farm. She often traveled far to help the sick or deliver a child.

Finally Minoka-Hill borrowed the $100 fee and got her Wisconsin license in 1934. Even so, she never charged more for treatment than a patient could afford. In 1947 the Oneida Tribe adopted their beloved doctor. A monument in her honor was erected after her death.

Lady Mary Montagu (1689–1762)
Pioneer in smallpox vaccination, writer

DR. EDWARD JENNER INTRODUCED THE SMALLPOX vaccination in 1798, but the first step toward eradicating this serious disease was initiated by Lady Mary Wortley Montagu 80 years earlier. Smallpox, which is caused by a virus, spreads very easily. Before it was possible to control it, epidemics occurred regularly, and about 30 percent of the people who caught it died. Survivors were often permanently scarred.

Lady Montagu belonged to a noble British family and knew many of the literary celebrities of her day. In 1716, newly recovered from smallpox, she traveled to Turkey, where her husband, Edward, was an ambassador. There she observed elderly women performing a folk cure. Using a procedure known as inoculation, they scraped the skin of a

healthy child and applied tissue from a mild case of smallpox to the cut. After a few days of low fever, the child was immune to the disease.

Once she was back home in England, Lady Montagu arranged demonstrations of the method. First, to gain people's trust, she performed the procedure on her daughter. Then, with the backing of Caroline, Princess of Wales, six prisoners and six orphans were successfully inoculated. The method became popular, and the mortality rate from smallpox dropped to two percent.

Today Lady Montagu is still famous for her witty published letters and essays. It's less well known that she not only saved lives, she helped people accept the notion of inoculation.

Sushila Nayar (1914–)
Physician

SUSHILA NAYAR WAS BORN IN GUJARAT, PAKISTAN. She went to Lahore College for Women and to the Lady Hardinge Medical College in Delhi, as well as Johns Hopkins University in Baltimore, Maryland.

Nayar was a follower of the political activist Mahatma Gandhi from the time she was a teenager, supporting his dream of an India that was free from the colonial rule of the British. As a young doctor, she worked as Gandhi's personal physician, and she spent two years in prison as a result of her involvement with his cause.

After India became independent in 1947, Nayar held several government positions and became involved in public health organizations. From 1952 to 1956 she was speaker of the Delhi Legislative Assembly. She was appointed minister of health in 1962 and served for five years. She was chair of the Indian Red Cross and was active in the Tuberculosis Association of India. In 1969 she was appointed director of the Mahatma Gandhi Institute of Medical Sciences.

Margaret Morse Nice (1883–1974)
Ornithologist

MARGARET MORSE NICE WAS TECHNICALLY AN "amateur" ornithologist, but her research added significantly to knowledge about birds. She was so well respected among her fellow scientists that they elected her president of the Wilson Ornithological Society in 1938 and 1939.

Growing up in Amherst, Massachusetts, the 12-year-old Nice had her own paper, *Fruit Acre News*, in which she often wrote about birds. Later, after studying at Mount Holyoke College and Clark University, she published a paper, "The Food of the Bob-White" (1910), the first of many scientific writings. She had spent over two years observing bobwhites, and her meticulous work was well received. In another groundbreaking study, she observed the personalities of individual song sparrows in their natural habitat.

While many scientists have research assistants and secretaries, Nice worked alone from her home—and raised five daughters. When they were small, she studied psychology and wrote articles about children's development, although she never stopped observing birds. After 1936 she and her husband, Blaine, lived in Chicago, where she worked to educate the public about environmental issues. In 1969 the Wilson Ornithological Society established the Margaret Morse Nice Grant to support amateur ornithologists.

Antonia Novello (1944–)
Surgeon General of the United States

TWO FORCES INFLUENCED ANTONIA NOVELLO to become a doctor. The first was her mother, a school principal, who raised Antonia and her brother in Puerto Rico after their father died. The second was her painful experience with a congenital intestinal disease. The condition was corrected by surgery when she was 18. By then she had decided to learn to help others.

After earning her M.D. in 1970, Novello became a kidney disease specialist at the University of Michigan Medical Center in Ann Arbor. Her frustration with a system that prevented many patients from obtaining transplants led her to public health administration.

She worked with several national health organizations and, in 1990, President George Bush appointed her Surgeon General of the United States.

First Novello focused on children's health. She campaigned to discourage drinking and smoking among teenagers, meeting with beer and wine companies to persuade them to stop advertising to minors. Health-care reform for women and minorities was another priority. She was concerned about the lack of AIDS awareness in the heterosexual community. And she pointed out that, in the Hispanic and Latino community, the tuberculosis rate is four times higher than the country's average.

Novello served three years as Surgeon General. She continues her public health work as a UNICEF representative and through writing and lecturing.

Christiane Nüsslein-Volhard (1942–)
Geneticist, biologist

CHRISTIANE NÜSSLEIN-VOLHARD'S FATHER WAS AN architect, and her mother came from a long line of artists. Their home in Frankfurt, Germany, was filled with artistic creativity. Christiane, with her fascination for science, felt a little out of place. But she knew what she wanted. By 1995 she had been named one of three winners of the Nobel Prize for medicine.

In the late 1970s, Nüsslein-Volhard began working with a future fellow prizewinner, Eric Wieschaus, studying the development of a single-cell egg into a living thing. They could observe as the egg multiplied into more cells, but they wondered how each of those cells knew to develop into the correct part of the body. One of their important discoveries was that development is controlled by a code from the mother's genes. Their research led to an international effort to map all of the genes for other life forms, especially humans. This can help scientists understand more about birth defects. The laboratory techniques Nüsslein-Volhard and Wieschaus developed are now used worldwide.

Nüsslein-Volhard has spent most of her career working at the Max-Planck Institute for Developmental Biology in Tübingen. Since 1990 she has been director of the Department of Genetics there.

Eleanor Anne Ormerod (1828–1901)
Economic entomologist

As a girl Eleanor Ormerod explored her father's estate in Gloucestershire, England, and developed a love for natural sciences. On her own, she read about entomology, the study of insects, and became an authority. She was not only interested in unusual and specialized facts; she loved to apply her knowledge in a common-sense way to everyday problems. In doing so, she revolutionized agriculture.

Ormerod began publishing her *Annual Report of Injurious Insects* in 1877. The free reports, with contributions from scientists all over the world, gave farmers uncomplicated advice about how to control harmful insects. For example, to get rid of maggots that threatened cows, she suggested "a dab of cart grease and sulphur." The remedy solved the problem, saving thousands of animals.

She also understood the interaction of living things. When a farmer asked her to find out why one of his watercress crops had mysteriously failed, she discovered that his wife loved herons and had attracted them to the property. The herons had eaten too many trout, which normally consumed insects— leaving the insects free to devour the watercress.

Generous with her expertise and sought-after as a speaker, Ormerod received many honors during her lifetime. She did not retire until four months before her death.

Angeliki Panajiotatou (1875–1954)
Microbiologist

Following in the footsteps of one of her countrywomen from ancient times, Artemisia, Queen of Caria, Angeliki Panajiotatou resolved to study medicine. She was accepted at Athens University's medical school, where she and her sister were the first women students. Angeliki spent time studying in Germany, too. Then she returned home to teach at Athens University. At her first class, the students—all men—shouted at her to go back to the kitchen. When they refused to attend her lectures, she resigned.

Cairo University in Egypt offered Panajiotatou a job. Before long, she became director of the hospital in Alexandria, where she specialized in tropical diseases, typhus, and cholera. She spent 30 years in Egypt, and her work was internationally renowned.

Panajiotatou kept in touch with Greek friends, who told her that women scientists were beginning to gain acceptance there. Finally, in 1938, she returned to Athens and was immediately offered a position at the university. This time no one refused to attend her classes.

Elsie Worthington Clews Parsons (1875–1941)
Anthropologist, sociologist

Elsie Parsons's first book, *The Family* (1906), was so controversial that she published her next book under the pseudonym John Main. Her husband, Herbert, was a politician, and she didn't want to ruin his chances for election. In *The Family* she argued for equal opportunities for men and women. Particularly shocking was the fact that she advocated "trial marriages."

In 1915, on a visit to the Southwest, Parsons became interested in Native American cultures. Although she already had her Ph.D. in sociology, she began studying anthropology with Franz Boas. Soon she was researching several different tribes, including the Zuni and the Pueblo. Parsons focused on recording her observations and analyzing them. She

often used examples from Native American cultures to show how society's expectations affected individual behavior. Over the years she expanded her studies to include the folklore of several different island communities. She was president of the American Folklore Society and editor of the *Journal of American Folklore*. The noted anthropologist Ruth Benedict was one of her students when she taught at the New School for Social Research in New York.

Parsons's progressive views stood in sharp contrast to her conservative, society upbringing. A pacifist, she wrote for the radical magazine *The Masses* and was among the intellectuals who gathered in Greenwich Village. Even with her career of travel and scholarship, Parsons maintained a family life that included three children.

Edith Patch (1876–1954)
Entomologist

EVEN EDITH PATCH, A DEDICATED FIELD-WORKER, thought twice about spending the summer in a potato field in Maine. But she had to do it to prove that potato aphids were responsible for ruining the crop. Her theory was that the aphids laid their eggs on wild rosebushes and remained there over the winter. The eggs hatched in the spring, in time to feed on the potato plants. Other entomologists challenged her theory, saying there were too few wild roses in the area. She found her evidence that summer, though, and convinced them.

Charles D. Woods of the University of Maine had recognized Patch's talents as an entomologist in 1903. First he asked her to work unpaid for nearly a year, setting up the university's entomology department. Then he gave her a salary and put her in charge, ignoring the sexist comments of other scientists.

Edith Patch wrote several technical books and articles, as well as science articles for the general public. In 1930 she became the first woman president of the Entomological Association of America. After retiring in 1937, she wrote 17 successful children's books about nature.

Ruth Patrick (1907–)
Limnologist, environmental scientist

DR. RUTH PATRICK ESTIMATES THAT HER WORK HAS taken her to 850 rivers around the world. She is a limnologist, a scientist who studies freshwater. She is also a famous expert in diatoms, algae that are made up of just one cell. Different species of diatoms

Global Warming

One of the issues that concerns Ruth Patrick is global warming. The Earth is kept warm enough for life to flourish through the "greenhouse effect," by which carbon dioxide molecules in the atmosphere trap heat from the Sun's rays near the Earth's surface—much the way the windows of a greenhouse hold the Sun's warmth inside the structure. But if the amount of gas in the atmosphere is increased, the Earth could become too warm, disrupting the world's ecosystems. Modern society relies heavily on fossil fuels, such as oil and coal, which, when burned, emit carbon dioxide. Patrick supports the development of alternative—clean—energy sources that may help to halt this dangerous process.

thrive in different environments. Therefore, the variety, size, and number of diatoms in a body of water provide a way to assess the health of that water. Patrick created a method to grow diatoms for research and invented a "diatometer," for plotting their size and growth.

Patrick's father had encouraged her interest in science, taking her on nature walks around their home in Topeka, Kansas, and giving the seven-year-old girl a microscope. She earned her Ph.D. from the University of Virginia in 1934. Then, because of its superb collection of diatoms, she began working at the Academy of Natural Sciences in Philadelphia. In 1947 she established the academy's limnology department and led it for more than 40 years.

Patrick has served as an adviser to the Environmental Protection Agency, the Renewable Resources Foundation, and other groups. She helped to draft the Clean Water Act of 1972, which provided for regulating the discharge of wastewater and for establishing water treatment facilities. Her numerous honors include the 1975 John and Alice Tyler Ecology Award and the National Medal of Science, presented to her in 1996 by President Bill Clinton.

Mary Engle Pennington (1872–1952)
Food scientist, chemist, refrigeration specialist

BEFORE FOOD GETS TO OUR HOMES, IT IS KEPT refrigerated in warehouses, trucks, and grocery stores. Otherwise, it would spoil. In the early 1900s, though, keeping foods cool was a new and complicated idea. Mary Pennington developed food preservation techniques that have probably saved thousands of people from food poisoning.

Pennington entered the University of Pennsylvania in 1892. In two years she completed all the work for a degree, but since she was a woman, the university only gave her a certificate of proficiency. She continued her studies anyway, and in 1895, received her Ph.D. without dispute.

Pennington started her own laboratory, where she analyzed tissue samples for local doctors. Soon she had a top-notch reputation. She became a lecturer at the Woman's Medical College of Pennsylvania and worked with the city's health department. Her research on preserving milk helped establish national health inspection standards. In 1907 she applied for a job at the Department of Agriculture, using the

A Scientist Rides the Rails

Probably the best known of Mary Pennington's many projects was undertaken during World War I. She designed refrigerated railroad cars so that food could be shipped safely from farms to markets. Many times she rode the trains to monitor the performance of the machinery—and was amused when rumors circulated that she traveled *in* the chilly refrigerated chambers with the cargo.

name M. E. Pennington, so they wouldn't reject her just because of her sex. Once there, she developed new techniques for food handling and convinced the food industries to adopt them. She improved refrigeration by inventing a way of controlling moisture so that food did not get too dried out or moldy.

Dr. Pennington received many awards, including the Notable Service Medal for her work on preserving food during shipping. She had no interest in retiring and continued working until she died at age 80.

Susan La Flesche Picotte (1865–1915)
Physician

SUSAN LA FLESCHE RECEIVED HER EARLY EDUCATION in the government schools on the Omaha Indian Reservation in Nebraska. Like her sister, Susette, who became famous as the American Indian rights activist Bright Eyes, she later attended boarding school in the East. A brilliant student, she received a scholarship from the Women's National Indian Association to attend the Woman's Medical College of Pennsylvania.

Susan was hired in 1890 to work as a doctor at the

government school on the reservation where she was born. It wasn't long before she was treating all the members of her tribe. She traveled by horseback, often in difficult conditions, to see her patients.

In 1894 she married Henry Picotte, but Susan continued practicing medicine. Her husband died in 1905 of an alcohol-related illness, leaving her to raise their two sons alone. Temperance had been an important cause to Susan's father, the tribe's chief. Now she took it up, too, traveling to Washington, D.C., in 1906 and successfully lobbying for laws to ban alcohol sales on the Winnebago and Omaha reservations.

Although her leadership was unofficial, in practice, Picotte was the spokesperson for her tribe. Among her many accomplishments was the establishment of a hospital in Walthill, Nebraska. After her death from a painful bone infection, the hospital was renamed in her honor.

Hortense Powdermaker (1896–1970)
Anthropologist

HORTENSE POWDERMAKER DISCOVERED HER interest in anthropology in 1925 while studying abroad at the London School of Economics. Her teacher, Bronislaw Malinowski, influenced her career with his theories about psychoanalysis in relation to anthropology. Studying anthropology felt comfortable to Powdermaker, who had, as a Jew growing up in Pennsylvania and Baltimore, already taken notice of social classes and prejudice.

Race in the United States was a frequent topic for Powdermaker. While working for the Institute of Human Relations at Yale University, she conducted one of the first anthropological studies of a community in the United States. Her research in Indianola, Mississippi, focused on social issues in the town's African American and white communities. In 1944 she addressed the topic of race for high school students in her book *Probing Our Prejudices*. Later she began researching media and

society. In her most famous book, *Hollywood, The Dream Factory* (1950), she analyzed the values of the filmmaking industry and how they affected the types of movies made.

Dr. Powdermaker was a popular teacher at Queens College in New York, where she worked for 30 years. While there, she founded a program combining anthropology and sociology. She enjoyed her work with students and was good at helping others discover the excitement of anthropology. Her final book, *Stranger and Friend: The Way of an Anthropologist* (1966), tells the story of her career.

Ann Preston (1813–1872)
Physician, educator

ANN PRESTON WAS RAISED IN A QUAKER FAMILY that supported women's rights and opposed slavery. She spent two years in a medical apprenticeship. In 1849 she applied without success to the four medical schools in Philadelphia.

The next year a group of Quakers established the Female (later Woman's) Medical College of Pennsylvania. Preston spent the rest of her career there, first as a student, then as a professor and administrator. The Philadelphia Medical Society denounced the college, making it impossible for graduates to get internships at teaching hospitals. So, in 1861, Preston helped found the Woman's Hospital, where her students could complete the practical side of their education.

As dean of the Woman's Medical College after 1866, Preston convinced some Philadelphia hospitals to accept women as interns at their clinics. Male students held demonstrations against them, claiming it was immoral for men and women to study medicine together. Dr. Preston's eloquent response to their concerns appeared in Philadelphia newspapers on November 15, 1869.

Margie Profet (1958–)
Biologist

MARGIE PROFET CAME TO STUDY BIOLOGY IN an unusual way. She began by majoring in political philosophy at Harvard University. After graduating in 1980, she traveled in Europe and worked as a computer programmer. Then she earned a second undergraduate degree—this time in physics—at the University of California in Berkeley, her hometown.

Profet did not go on to graduate school. Instead she began spending time in the library, researching whatever interested her. Prompted by her own itchy reactions to certain soaps, she wondered what purpose allergies served. Her research suggested that they might be the body's way of protecting itself from toxic substances. Her paper explaining this theory appeared in the *Quarterly Review of Biology* in 1991 and attracted scientists' attention, although many were skeptical.

In 1993 Profet published another paper, theorizing that the purpose of menstruation was to rid a woman's body of bacteria carried by sperm. Again, her ideas were controversial, but her thought-provoking work was appreciated. That year Profet was awarded a MacArthur Foundation Fellowship. This "genius grant" provides the recipient with $250,000 to fund any project that interests her. Since then, Profet has focused on pregnancy and ways to prevent birth defects.

Mamphela Ramphele (1948–)
Physician, activist

D R. MAMPHELA RAMPHELE GREW UP IN THE Transvaal province of South Africa, the daughter of teachers. She was one of the first black South African women to receive an M.D. from the University of Natal. While there, she fell in love with Steve Biko, a leader in the antiapartheid movement.

Ramphele helped set up the Zanempilo Health Clinic at King William's Town in 1975. Two years later, because of her relationship with Biko, she was banished to the northern Transvaal. Biko was imprisoned and murdered while in custody, an event that made international headlines. After the news reached Ramphele in exile, she took solace in the birth of their son, Hlumelo, and in her work. Perceiving a dire need for health services in her new community, Ramphele turned an old shopping center into a clinic. She also created a day-care center, a library, and a scholarship fund. When Ramphele's exile was lifted six years later, she stayed until a doctor could be found to replace her.

Ramphele moved to Cape Town and began teaching at the university, where she was appointed vice-chancellor in 1996. She is the author of several books, including *Across Boundaries: The Journey of a South African Woman Leader* (1997).

Mary Jane Rathbun (1860–1943)
Marine zoologist

L IKE OTHER WOMEN SCIENTISTS OF HER DAY, MARY Jane Rathbun spent time at the Woods Hole Marine Biological Station in Massachusetts. Her older brother Richard, assistant to the head of the United States Fish Commission, first brought her there in 1881. Captivated by the work, she spent the several summers cataloging the marine animals that were brought in on survey ships.

In 1884 she was hired at the National Museum in Washington, D.C., and became a clerk in the department of marine invertebrates in 1886. She participated in every aspect of the department, from writing correspondence to maintaining the library. Essentially, she was the curator of the division, although that title belonged to Richard. He gave her credit for her many roles in his reports to the museum's board.

Rathbun became a noted expert on decapod crustaceans—marine animals, such as crabs and shrimp, that have a hard exoskeleton and five pairs of leglike appendages. Most of her 158 publications focused on the organization and scientific naming of *Crustacea*. Although she gave up her salary in 1914 so that an assistant could be paid, Rathbun stayed at the museum for over 50 years. She helped continue her work by leaving $10,000 to the Smithsonian Institution in her will.

Miriam Louisa Rothschild (1908–)
Zoologist, entomologist

BORN INTO AN ILLUSTRIOUS BANKING FAMILY, Miriam Rothschild grew up on her father's estate, Ashton Wold, in England. A love for the natural sciences is one of the legacies of being a Rothschild. Her father donated his flea collection to the British Museum. Her uncle, Lionel Walter, opened his own museum to display a collection that included 2.25 million butterflies and 200,000 bird eggs.

Primarily self-educated, Rothschild has explored many different topics and written or coauthored over 300 works. She is probably best known for her study of fleas. Between 1953 and 1974, she catalogued and illustrated the 30,000 fleas in her father's collection, a work that filled six volumes. Her research on how fleas jump showed that the tiny creatures have ligaments and muscles similar to those of insects that can fly.

Plant poisons and insects also interested Rothschild. She discovered that monarch caterpillars evolved a resistance to poisons in the milkweed plants they eat. This means most predators avoid

"A parasite's life is an impressive gamble. Indeed it is difficult to envisage insecurity on such a scale. The chances of a grouse roundworm finding a grouse are far less than the reader's chances of becoming the parent of quads, or a cabinet minister."

MIRIAM ROTHSCHILD
Fleas, Flukes & Cuckoos, 1952

them. Her interest in butterflies inspired her to design gardens to attract the beautiful creatures.

In addition to her scientific studies, Rothschild has maintained her family's tradition of helping others. Among her many causes, she has supported research on schizophrenia, the humane treatment of animals, and free meals for schoolchildren.

Florence Rena Sabin (1871–1953)
Physician, anatomist, educator

IN 1896 FLORENCE SABIN WAS ONE OF THE FIRST women to enroll at the medical school at Johns Hopkins University in Baltimore, Maryland. She would spend over 25 years there, first as a student, then as a researcher and teacher. Early on, she met Franklin P. Mall, a professor of anatomy who became her mentor and colleague.

Sabin's research focused on the lymphatic and blood systems. She discovered that the lymph system, an important component of human response to disease, originates from the veins rather than the surrounding tissue, as was previously believed. In 1902 Sabin became the first woman accepted to the medical school faculty at Hopkins. She was an energetic, popular teacher who allowed her students to discover information for themselves, rather than requiring them to memorize it. Despite all her

accomplishments, one of Dr. Sabin's former male students was chosen over her to be chair of the anatomy department in 1917.

Sabin left Johns Hopkins in 1925 and became the first woman member of the Rockefeller Institute in New York City. During her 13 years there, she studied the cell's role in fighting diseases, focusing especially on tuberculosis.

In 1944, six years after she had retired to her home state of Colorado, the 73-year-old Sabin agreed to serve on a public health committee convened by Governor John Vivian. Distressed when her surveys showed the state's health policies to be terribly inadequate, she began a crusade to reform them, and kept it up until the end of her life. As in all her enterprises, her energy, ability to communicate, and clarity of focus served her well.

Kate Olivia Sessions (1857–1940)
Horticulturist

VISITORS TO SAN DIEGO NOTICE THE BEAUTIFUL trees and plants, but they probably don't know that the person responsible for cultivating most of them was Kate Sessions. A California native, Sessions grew up in Oakland and moved to San Diego after graduating from the University of California at Berkeley in 1881. She began working as a teacher but left after four years to open a plant nursery. It was the beginning of a long and influential career in horticulture.

Looking to expand her nursery business in 1892, Sessions negotiated a lease with the city of San Diego for 30 acres (12 ha) of land. She agreed to plant 100 trees on the land and donate 300 trees to the city every year. In addition to filling the neighborhoods with unusual trees, her work resulted in Balboa Park, an oasis of plants, trees, and open space. She traveled around the world, searching for seeds and plants to cultivate.

Sessions published over 250 articles on horticulture. She helped found the San Diego Floral Association in 1909 and initiated the City's Arbor Day Celebrations. From 1915 to 1918, she returned to work at schools, this time as a supervisor of agriculture. Among her many honors was the naming of an elementary school after her in 1956.

Anna Nikitichna Shabanova (1848–1932)
Pediatrician

EVEN THOUGH SHE WAS BORN INTO A WEALTHY Russian family, Anna Shabanova developed an early awareness of the sufferings of the working class. In 1866 she was sent to prison for six months for organizing a dressmakers' cooperative in Moscow. Once released, she decided to become a doctor and enrolled at the new Women's Medical Academy in Helsinki, Finland. She focused on pediatrics, the study of children's diseases.

Returning home to Russia, Shabanova taught medicine, wrote, and continued to participate in political activities. Between 1905 and 1917, she led the suffrage division of the Mutual Philanthropic Society, an organization involved in education and helping to alleviate social problems.

Shabanova was particularly active in relief organizations during World War I. As a member of the War Industries Committee, she met the British suffragist Emmeline Pankhurst during her visit to Moscow. Renewed peace allowed Shabanova to return her focus to medicine. She published her final book on pediatrics in 1926.

Jane Sharp (17th century)
Midwife

ALTHOUGH FEW DETAILS OF JANE SHARP'S LIFE are known, her influential textbook _The Midwives' Book; or The Whole Art of Midwifery Discovered_ (1671), was the first manual of its kind written by an Englishwoman. In it, Sharp conveyed the knowledge and opinions she had acquired in a career that lasted over 30 years. She criticized the growing trend for men to attend women at childbirth, feeling that helping to deliver babies should be the job of women. Women were denied the advantage of a university education, she admitted, but she emphasized that they could learn their craft just as well by studying with other practitioners.

Sharp covered a range of topics in her book, from male and female anatomy to the stages of pregnancy. She recommended a proper diet and exercise to maintain good health. Superior manuals could be found in other countries at the time, but Jane Sharp's text was comprehensive and practical, among the best available in England.

Regina von Siebold (1771–1849)
Charlotte von Siebold (1788–1859)
Physicians

A MOTHER-AND-DAUGHTER PROFESSIONAL TEAM, the von Siebolds were respected physicians in early 19th-century Germany. Regina Henning was widowed at a young age, but her second husband, Damien von Siebold, adopted her daughter, Charlotte, in 1795 and raised her as his own. Damien was the court physician at Darmstadt, and Regina became his assistant. She also studied obstetrics privately.

By 1807 Regina was given permission to practice obstetrics and administer vaccinations on her own. Eight years later she became the first woman awarded a doctorate from the University of Giessen. In the meantime, Charlotte had been following her mother's lead. She earned her medical degree from Giessen in 1817 and studied anatomy, physiology, and pathology at the University of Göttingen. The women shared a medical practice in Darmstadt for several years.

Charlotte became so well known that she often attended royal births. Her assistance was particularly requested by the Duke and Duchess of Kent when the duchess gave birth to a daughter in 1819. Three months later, Charlotte delivered a little boy for the Duchess of Coburg. That little girl eventually became Queen Victoria of England, and the boy grew up to be Prince Albert, Victoria's husband.

Maud Caroline Slye (1869–1954)
Pathologist

WHEN SHE STARTED OUT, MAUD SLYE EARNED SO little money that she sometimes went without food so that her mice could eat. Mice were central to her research. She studied hundreds of thousands of them in developing her theories on inheritance as a factor in cancer.

Slye was born to educated but impoverished parents in Minneapolis, Minnesota. She paid her tuition to the University of Chicago for three years by working full-time as a secretary and studying whenever she could. But this schedule was terribly stressful. She eventually had a breakdown and, after a brief rest, completed her degree in 1899 at Brown University in Rhode Island.

After teaching for several years, Slye returned to the University of Chicago in 1908 to work in a laboratory. It was there that she began her research on cancer using mice. Many scientists thought cancer might be inherited, but there was no research to support this theory until Slye provided it. She also discovered that it was not contagious.

Slye theorized that the type of cancer was determined by one gene and the location of the tumor was determined by another gene. Today scientists know that the issue is far more complicated, but they agree that an individual's chance of getting cancer is much greater if a relative has had it.

Nettie Maria Stevens (1861–1912)
Geneticist, biologist

IN THE LATE 1800S, SCIENTISTS UNDERSTOOD THAT traits were passed on from parent to offspring, but a direct relationship between chromosomes and heredity hadn't been determined. Nettie Maria Stevens confirmed this link when she discovered that the sex of an organism was determined by X and Y chromosomes, rather than the effect of environmental factors on the developing cells. She announced her discovery in 1905, and received the Ellen Richards Prize for her work. Later that year the same discovery was made independently by Edmund Beecher Wilson at Columbia University.

Stevens didn't even go to college until she was 35 years old. After years of working as a teacher and librarian in Massachusetts, she decided to go to Stanford University in California. She spent her summer vacations studying at the Hopkins Seaside Laboratory and soon became interested in the study of cells and their parts. Eventually, she began researching a group of microscopic organisms called ciliate protozoa.

In 1900 she began her Ph.D. work at Bryn Mawr in Pennsylvania, where, aside from several fellowships abroad, she spent the rest of her career. Her work turned to investigating cell development in embryos and eventually to chromosomes. She was studying chromosomes in insects when she died of breast cancer at the age of 50.

Emily Jennings Stowe (1831–1903)
Physician

EMILY STOWE WANTED TO BECOME A DOCTOR, but she was denied entrance to Canadian medical schools. Over a decade after Elizabeth Blackwell had become the United States' first woman doctor, Canadian schools were still not accepting women.

Emily Jennings married John Stowe in 1856. By then she had already spent nearly a decade teaching in Ontario schools. Intent on changing careers and becoming a doctor, she went to the United States after Canadian schools rejected her. In 1867 she graduated from the New York College of Medicine for Women.

Back home in Canada, Dr. Stowe was still not accepted by the Ontario College of Physicians and Surgeons, which conferred official permission to practice. She saw patients illegally for years. At last, in 1880, she became the first woman in Canada to receive a medical license. Stowe was also active in the women's suffrage movement. She founded the Toronto Women's Literacy Club to promote women's rights and was president of the Dominion Women's Enfranchisement Association from 1889 until her death. Her daughter, Augusta Stowe Gullen, was the first woman in the country who received an M.D. from a Canadian university.

Miranda Stuart (1795?–1865)
Physician

DURING HER LIFE MIRANDA STUART WOULD never have been included in a book on women scientists—because everyone thought she was a man. Under the alias James Barry, Stuart kept

her secret until it was discovered at her death. Even then many tried to deny it, fearing it would support the fight for women to become doctors.

The details of her birth in England and childhood are not known. James Barry graduated from the Edinburgh School of Medicine in 1812. This was the same school where, over 50 years later, Elizabeth Garrett Anderson and Sophia Jex-Blake revolutionized women's role in medicine. Barry became a surgeon for the British Army. She spent several years working in South Africa before being appointed the inspector-general of Canadian hospitals in 1857.

Dr. Barry was considered a brilliant surgeon. In 1826 she saved a woman from dying during childbirth by performing a cesarean section. This was the first time in South Africa that both mother and child had survived that operation. She angered many authorities with her demands for better medical treatment for women, prisoners, and the mentally ill. She was, in fact, never shy about expressing her opinions and even fought in more than one duel during her lifetime.

Helen Brooke Taussig (1898–1986)
Pediatric cardiologist

BEFORE DR. HELEN TAUSSIG BEGAN HER WORK, "blue baby" syndrome (so-called because the infant is born cyanotic, or with a blue tinge to the skin) was usually fatal. Taussig suspected the condition was caused by a defect of the pulmonary artery, which carries blood from the heart to the lungs, and she had an idea for repairing the artery. However, as a cardiologist, she did not perform surgery. In 1941 she began working with the surgeon Alfred Blalock. Three years later, using a technique that is now called the Blalock-Taussig method, he successfully corrected the defect in a newborn baby.

Taussig began studying medicine in 1921. She started at Harvard University in her hometown of Cambridge, even though she knew they wouldn't grant a degree to a woman. But after she was refused permission to study anatomy, she transferred to Boston University. The dean of the medical school suggested she go to Johns Hopkins in Baltimore, where women had been admitted for over 20 years.

Finally, she finished her degree at Hopkins, and spent the rest of her career as a researcher and teacher there.

In 1962, after hearing that unusually many babies were being born with serious deformities in Europe, she went to investigate. She determined that thalidomide, a new sleeping pill that the mothers had taken while pregnant, was responsible. Taussig warned the United States Food and Drug Administration, and, because of her vigilance, thalidomide was never approved for use in America.

Lucy Beaman Hobbs Taylor (1833–1910)
Dentist

LUCY HOBBS WAS ABLE TO START PRACTICING before she had a degree, because dentists weren't yet required to have licenses. Not that she hadn't tried to get official certification. As a woman, her applications to medical and dental schools had all been denied. She studied privately instead. Dentistry was still a young science, and much of her education involved learning to administer anesthesia and construct false teeth.

Raised in New York State, Hobbs moved to the Midwest, became interested in medicine, and turned to dentistry on the recommendation of her physician tutor. By 1865 she had a practice in McGregor, Iowa. That year she was elected to the Iowa State Dental Society and represented them at the American Dental Association's meeting in Chicago. Her improved status convinced the Ohio College of Dental Surgery—which had rejected her four years earlier—to accept her as a student. She received the first dentistry degree awarded to an American woman in 1866.

Hobbs married James Taylor in 1867. She taught him dentistry, and they practiced together in Lawrence, Kansas, for 20 years.

Mary Harris Thompson (1829–1895)
Physician, surgeon

MARY THOMPSON PAID HER WAY THROUGH boarding school and college by teaching a variety of scientific classes. In preparation for teaching anatomy and physiology, she studied in Boston at the New England Female Medical College and enjoyed it so much that she decided to become a doctor. After two years in Boston and a yearlong

internship with the Blackwell sisters in New York City, she received her M.D. in 1863.

The large cities on the east coast already had women doctors, so Thompson moved to Chicago. There, she cofounded the Chicago Hospital for Women and Children and became head of the medical and surgical staff. In 1870, after advanced training, she received a diploma from the Chicago Medical College. As soon as she left, though, the administrators gave in to complaints by male students and refused other female applicants. In response Thompson helped establish the Woman's Hospital Medical College.

Known for her surgical skill and admired for her dedication to treating the poor, Thompson was elected vice-president of the Chicago Medical Society in 1881. Just as she had set out to do, Thompson paved the way for women in medicine, especially in the midwestern states.

Trotula of Salerno (late 11th century)
Physician

TROTULA, A PHYSICIAN WHO LIVED IN MEDIEVAL Italy, is the only member of the *Mulieres Salernitanae*, or the "Ladies of Salerno," whose writings have survived. The *Mulieres* were respected female practitioners who were associated with the university at Salerno, which was unique for its time. Not only were women admitted, it was the first medical center that was not connected with the Catholic church.

Trotula advocated preventative medicine, encouraging all her patients to exercise, eat properly, and practice good hygiene. She used massage, herbs, and baths for treatment and was one of the first physicians who did not rely on astrology, superstition, or prayer. Her work in women's health was especially important, and her techniques for assisting in childbirth were revolutionary.

Trotula was the first person to write specifically on women's health needs, most significantly in *Passionibus Mulierum Curandorum* (The Diseases of Women). Her writings were used for centuries, passed down in handwritten copies. Unfortunately, in the copying process her work was often credited to a different author or signed with a male version of her name.

Lillias Stirling Horton Underwood (1851–1921)
Physician, Presbyterian missionary

EVER SINCE HER CHILDHOOD IN ALBANY, NEW York, Lillias Horton had intended to become a missionary. Her mother had strongly encouraged it. As a young woman, she volunteered at Chicago hospitals and was inspired to become a doctor, as well. She graduated from the Woman's Medical College of Chicago in 1887. The following year the Presbyterian Board of Foreign Missions sent her to Seoul, Korea.

In Seoul Horton directed the women's department and the dispensary at the government hospital. She was also the personal physician to Queen Min, an influential association that she maintained until the queen's assassination in 1895. In 1889 she married Horace Grant Underwood, a missionary clergyman.

In 1893 Underwood and her husband established a shelter, where they treated people suffering from infectious diseases. During the cholera epidemic of 1895, an impressive two-thirds of their patients survived. The conditions the Underwoods lived in were physically trying. Horace died of a tropical disease in 1916. Lillias herself suffered from rheumatic fever and arthritis, but she remained active and was working in Seoul at the time of her death.

Esther Boise Van Deman (1862–1937)
Archaeologist

IN 1907 ESTHER VAN DEMAN WENT TO A LECTURE in the Atrium Vestae in Rome. She noticed that the brickwork in one blocked doorway differed from that in other areas of the structure and wondered if those differences could help determine when the various parts of the building were constructed. A classical literature scholar as well as an archaeologist, Van Deman developed methods for dating building materials and compared her findings to ancient written accounts. She published *The Atrium Vestae* in 1909 and continued the work for the rest of her life. Many techniques that she devised are still in use.

Before she went to Rome, the Ohio-born Van Deman taught classics at several colleges, including Wellesley and Mount Holyoke in Massachusetts. Between jobs she continued her education, earning a Ph.D. from the University of Chicago in 1898. A fellowship from the American School of Classical Studies brought her to Italy in 1901.

Van Deman dreamed of publishing a comprehensive book about the dating of brick and concrete structures but never got around to it. In her last years, she arranged her notes so that a colleague, Marion E. Blake, could write the book instead. Van Deman is buried in Rome beneath a brick-and-concrete monument.

Bertha Van Hoosen (1863–1952)
Physician, surgeon, educator

BERTHA VAN HOOSEN OBTAINED HER M.D. FROM the University of Michigan in 1888 and embarked on an influential career. Her private practice in Chicago, which started slowly in 1892, flourished in just a few years. She was also a challenging and supportive teacher, who took special pride in mentoring women students—her "surgical daughters." In 1918 Van Hoosen became the first woman to direct a coeducational university medical department when she was appointed the head of obstetrics at Loyola University.

> "I had seen how . . . even a great career might be crushed under the strain of money. Accordingly, I vowed that money should never keep me from reaching my goal. I never kept a book or sent a bill during the first ten years of my practice, theorizing that patients belong to one of three classes: those whom no one could prevent paying their bills; those who never pay any bills, even under pressure; and those, to which group the vast majority of patients belong, who pay their bills if pleased with the service, and if it is humanly possible."
>
> **BERTHA VAN HOOSEN**
> *Petticoat Surgeon*, 1947

Van Hoosen, along with many feminists, was a proponent of pain relief during childbirth, although many American doctors opposed it. Between 1904 and 1908, she devised a combination injection of scopolamine and morphine that induced "twilight sleep," during which the mother felt no pain but remained awake for the birth.

Despite her professional success, Van Hoosen was angered by the discrimination she witnessed against women doctors. In 1915 she was the driving force behind the establishment of the American Medical Women's Association. Active until the end, she was 88 years old when she operated for the last time.

Mary Edwards Walker (1832–1919)
Physician, women's rights activist

MARY WALKER WAS BORN IN OSWEGO, NEW York, and trained at the Syracuse Medical College. An unsuccessful marriage to another doctor, Albert Miller, ended in divorce. When the Civil War began, she applied to be an army surgeon, but her request was denied, so she volunteered at the Patent Office Hospital. In 1862 she began working without approval in the tent hospitals in Virginia's battlefields. She was appointed assistant surgeon for the 52nd Ohio Regiment in Tennessee in 1863.

While crossing the Confederate line to treat civilians, Walker was captured and held for several months in Richmond, Virginia. After her release, she worked in a women's prison and an orphanage. She was awarded a Congressional Medal of Honor for her service. Her medal was one of many that were revoked in 1917 for lack of documentation, but she continued to wear it proudly.

Dr. Walker's ideas were progressive, but her increasing eccentricity alienated many people. For a time she took an active role in the suffrage movement, but then she rejected it. She explained that she could find no wording in the Constitution that explicitly forbade women to vote. Therefore they must already possess the right, she said—and she saw no reason to fight further. Women's dress reform attracted her attention early on. She enthusiastically wore bloomers, then adopted a soldier's uniform during the war, and, in later life, usually dressed as a man.

Margaret Floy Washburn (1871–1939)
Experimental psychologist

MARGARET FLOY WASHBURN TURNED TO experimental psychology as a way to accommodate her interest in both science and philosophy, which she studied as an undergraduate at Vassar College. She went on to do graduate work in psychology at Columbia University. But Columbia wouldn't accept a woman as a regular student, so she transferred to Cornell University and completed her Ph.D. in 1894. A decade later she returned to Vassar as a professor and researcher.

Much of Washburn's research focused on animal behavior, and in 1908 she published *The Animal Mind*. She also studied human responses, such as people's reactions to colors, or the different preferences expressed by poets and scientists for sounds in speech. Washburn involved her students in her research as subjects and collaborators. They were often credited as the coauthors of articles in her series, *Studies from the Psychological Laboratory of Vassar College*.

Washburn earned the respect of her peers by any standard, male or female. She was a member of the American Psychological Association and became its president in 1921. Ten years later, she was the second woman, after Florence Sabin, elected to the National Academy of Sciences. Washburn stayed at Vassar for over 30 years, retiring after she suffered a stroke in 1937.

Beatrice Potter Webb (1858–1943)
Economist, sociologist, social reformer

BEATRICE POTTER WAS RAISED IN A WEALTHY family in Gloucester, England. She was mostly self-educated and, in the late 1880s, began to research sweatshop labor. Her resulting articles established her as a social scientist. With her marriage to Sidney Webb in 1892, Beatrice found a perfect working partner.

The Webbs studied society using scientific methods. They published over 100 articles, books, and pamphlets about English society, government, and work. Beatrice took the lead in developing research questions and collecting the necessary data, while Sidney did the analysis. In 1894 they published their classic, *The History of Trade Unionism*. The next year the Webbs founded the London School of Economics to train social scientists.

Because of her scientific research, Beatrice was appointed to the Royal Commission on Poor Laws in 1905. Her *Minority Report of the Poor Law Commission* (1909) included her suggestions about changing laws and providing government support for the poor. Although the report was not immediately effective, it provided inspiration for future reforms.

Throughout their marriage, the Webbs were members of the socialist Fabian Society. In 1913, to express their views, they founded the *New Statesman*, still an important political magazine.

The Fabians advocated gradual social change rather than revolution, so when both Webbs decided to support the Communist government of the Soviet Union in their later years, many of their followers were confused by their dramatic change in philosophies. After Sidney died in 1947, the ashes of the couple were mixed and buried at Westminster Abbey in London, a high honor.

Ruth Westheimer (1928–)
Psychologist, media personality

KAROLA RUTH SEIGEL WAS BORN IN FRANKFURT, Germany. Because they were Jewish, her parents sent her to a Swiss school when she was 11 years old, to protect her from the Nazis. That year World War II began, and no one in Ruth's family survived. She moved to Israel and then to Paris, where she attended the Sorbonne and earned a psychology degree. Two early marriages ended in divorce. By 1961, when she married Fred Westheimer, she was living in New York City.

In 1970 Ruth Westheimer earned her Ph.D. in education from Columbia University and started teaching. Ten years later, she made a guest radio appearance to talk about her concept of "sexual literacy." The public loved her, and soon she had her own show to answer questions about sex. Now widely known as "Dr. Ruth," she is a television personality as well.

It is no surprise that Westheimer has critics: Some feel her subject is immoral, while others say she turns a serious topic into entertainment. She also has thousands of fans. Westheimer speaks in favor of marriage and family but also thinks sex education is important. Her answers are frank, humorous, and nonjudgmental. She has published several books, including *Dr. Ruth's Guide to Safer Sex* (1992).

Anna Wessels Williams (1863–1954)
Bacteriologist, public health physician

ANNA WILLIAMS BECAME FASCINATED WITH science as a schoolgirl, when she first looked through a teacher's microscope. Several years later her sister almost died during childbirth, so Anna resolved to become a doctor.

She graduated from the Woman's Medical College of the New York Infirmary in 1891, but practicing medicine was frustrating. So many diseases were incurable. In 1894 she began her career as a medical researcher with the New York City Department of Health, where, after 1905, she was assistant director of the lab.

Williams made important discoveries about several diseases, including scarlet fever, pneumonia, influenza, and rabies. Perhaps her most important work concerned diphtheria, an often fatal disease that causes inflammation of the heart and nervous system. The existing antitoxin was not very effective, so Williams isolated a new strain of the diphtheria germ and made a much more powerful antitoxin. The resulting immunization has prevented cases of diphtheria around the world.

Williams published many articles and books, including *Who's Who Among the Microbes* (1929), a guide for the public that explained why some germs were harmful while others could even be helpful. In 1936 Williams was honored at a dinner sponsored by the New York Women's Medical Society for her role in the advancement of women in medicine.

Preventing Rabies

Anna Williams did much to reduce the harm caused by rabies, a virus usually transmitted through the bite of an infected animal. Rabies causes abnormal behavior, paralysis, and death. On a visit to the Pasteur Institute in Paris in 1896, Williams obtained a rabies culture that yielded an effective vaccine. Next, she worked to hasten diagnosis; people who were infected had to be treated early. An Italian, Adelchi Negri, had found a distinctive cell in the brain tissue of rabid animals. Williams devised a way of staining tissue samples so the cell became visible more quickly.

Cicely Delphine Williams (1893–1992)
Public health physician, pediatrician

THE MEMBERS OF THE BRITISH COLONIAL OFFICE on the Gold Coast (now called Ghana), had long wanted a woman doctor on staff. They were overjoyed when Cicely Williams, a Jamaican who had trained at Oxford University, was posted there in 1929.

Soon Williams observed a worrisome disease that struck toddlers, causing swelling of the legs and stomach, a rash, and changed hair color. Because it occurred when a new baby was born in the family, Ghanaians called it the "weaning disease," *kwashiorkor*. Concluding that it must be a nutritional deficiency, Williams put the youngsters on a protein diet, and they soon returned to health.

Williams went on to work in many countries— 70 over the course of her career. She was held in a Japanese concentration camp in Singapore during World War II and nearly died of disease there. From 1948 to 1951, Williams was head of the child and maternal health section of the World Health Organization. Starting in 1955, she devoted herself to teaching and held posts at London University and Tulane University in New Orleans, Louisiana.

Dr. Williams received many honors, including recognition from the British Paediatric Association and the American Academy of Pediatrics. When she died one of her obituaries read, "The world's children are indebted to her."

Martha Wollstein (1868–1939)
Pathologist, pediatrician

DR. MARTHA WOLLSTEIN WAS A QUIET, INTENSELY private person whose colleagues rarely got to know her, and her outstanding work on childhood diseases is also less well known than it should be.

She attended the Woman's Medical College of the New York Infirmary and graduated in 1889. Wollstein then began working at Babies Hospital as a pathologist, a doctor studying the causes of diseases.

At first it was impossible to do experiments, because there was no laboratory. Then a wealthy biologist, Christian Herter, paid for the construction of a new facility in 1896, and Wollstein worked there until 1904, when she went to the Rockefeller Institute. In the course of her career, she investigated childhood leukemia, tuberculosis, polio, and pneumonia. She helped confirm that a dangerous type of infant diarrhea was caused by a disease—dysentery—rather than by poor nutrition. She worked on an effective treatment for meningitis and conducted experiments that helped establish that mumps was a virus, not a bacterial infection.

Dr. Wollstein passed on her careful methods to a generation of researchers. In 1930 she was the first woman invited into the American Pediatric Society.

Jane Cooke Wright (1919–)
Physician, cancer research specialist

JANE WRIGHT CAME FROM A FAMILY OF DOCTORS and pioneers. As African Americans, her father, grandfather, and uncle all overcame barriers to have careers in medicine. Her father, Louis Thompkins Wright, was a noted cancer researcher. Wright attended Smith College, where she was a record-breaking swimmer, then accepted a scholarship to New York Medical College. She graduated in 1945.

In 1949 Wright took a position at the Cancer Research Foundation at Harlem Hospital, where her father was director. Chemotherapy was in its early stages of development as a treatment for cancer, and Wright made many contributions to research in this field. After Louis's death in 1952, she took over his job.

In 1955 Wright began teaching at the New York University School of Medicine. Twelve years later, she returned to New York Medical College to become associate dean. She was the first African American woman to hold such a high university position. All the while she continued her study of cancer and chemotherapy. Dr. Wright was actively involved with numerous medical organizations, and was a

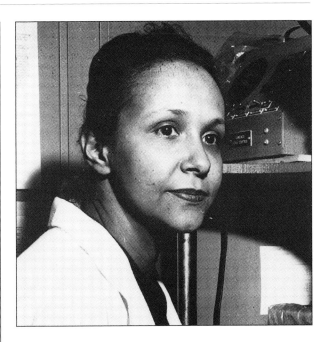

cofounder of the American Society for Clinical Oncology. She served on the President's Commission on Heart Disease, Cancer, and Stroke in 1964. In 1975 she was honored by the American Association for Cancer Research.

Rosalyn Yalow (1921–)
Medical physicist

ROSALYN YALOW, THE DAUGHTER OF JEWISH immigrants, had wanted to be a scientist since she was eight. She attended Hunter College in New York, then applied for graduate school. But every university turned her down because she was a woman. Then World War II began, and with many spots left vacant by soldiers, the University of Illinois decided to accept Yalow. She received her Ph.D. in 1945. Thirty-two years later, she became the second woman to win a Nobel Prize in medicine.

Yalow's Nobel Prize, which she shared with Andrew V. Schally and Roger Guillemin, was awarded for her development of radioimmunoassay, or RIA. The technique is used to detect tiny amounts of substances in the body. For example, Yalow used it to measure insulin in diabetic patients and learned a great deal about the disease. Today its many applications include checking donated blood for viruses and assessing the effectiveness of antibiotics.

While developing RIA, Yalow worked for 22 years with Solomon A. Berson at the Bronx Veterans Administration Hospital. His death in 1972 was devastating to her. Yalow also raised two children with her husband, Aaron. She never felt that she was sacrificing one role for another. As she said, "The world cannot afford the loss of the talents of half of its people if we are to solve the many problems which beset us."

Rachelle Slobodinsky Yarros (1869–1946)
Physician, social hygiene activist

LIKE MANY IMMIGRANTS TO THE UNITED STATES, Rachelle Slobodinsky's first job when she arrived from Russia was operating a sewing machine in a sweatshop. But she didn't stay there long. In 1890, at the encouragement of her future husband, Victor Yarros, she became the first woman admitted to the Boston College of Physicians and Surgeons. Moving to Philadelphia, she transferred to the Woman's Medical College of Pennsylvania and received her degree in 1893. Rachelle and Victor married the following year.

By 1895 they lived in Chicago at the social worker Jane Addams's Hull House, where they met many of the city's poor. That and her work in hospitals convinced Dr. Yarros that the sickness she treated in women was related to social conditions. Women knew too little about their bodies; they contracted diseases from uninformed sexual activity and endured too many pregnancies. Yarros began working to change laws and to provide public education. In 1914 she helped found the American Social Hygiene Association.

Like Margaret Sanger, Yarros advocated birth control. The clinic she opened in Chicago in 1923 was only the second of its kind in America. In 1933 she published *Modern Woman and Sex* to help change the public's attitude about women's place in society.

Marie Zakrzewska (1829–1902)
Physician, educator

MARIE ZAKRZEWSKA BECAME INTERESTED IN medicine while visiting her mother, who was studying to become a midwife at the Charité Hospital in Berlin. Marie was also accepted at the school and eventually became assistant to the director, Dr. Joseph Schmidt. In 1852, when Schmidt died, she took over his duties—as he had wished—but opposition to her role was strong. A year later, she immigrated to New York City, looking forward to greater acceptance of women in medicine.

Things weren't much better in America, but Zakrzewska did meet Dr. Elizabeth Blackwell, who encouraged her to attend Western Reserve University in Cleveland. She received her M.D. there in 1856. Returning to New York, she worked with Elizabeth and Emily Blackwell at their New York Infirmary for Women and Children. She then took a job on the faculty of the New England Female Medical College of Boston. But all her attempts to reform that foundering school were resisted, so she resigned. With the help of many supporters, she established the New England Hospital for Women and Children in 1863.

The new hospital, operated entirely by women, produced many of the best female doctors and nurses in the country. Knowing the public's prejudice against women doctors, Zakrzewska set high standards for the hospital training programs. She was also a supporter of women's suffrage and of the anti-slavery movement.

TIME LINE

Approximately 1400 B.C.E.	The Canaanites are defeated by the Israelites in the Siege of Jericho, an event described in the Bible's Old Testament. Nearly 1,600 years later, the British archaeologist Kathleen Kenyon will unearth evidence that the city was destroyed around that time.
6th century B.C.E.	The first books of the Old Testament are recorded.
Approximately 350 B.C.E.	Queen Artemisia II of Caria, known for her botanical and medical expertise as well as her political power, dies.
1st century	The books of the New Testament are written down.
390	Fabiola, a Roman noblewoman who has become a physician, cofounds a hospital at Porto.
622	In the Middle East, the prophet Mohammed is expelled from Mecca. He will become the founder of the Muslim religion.
Approximately 900	A medical school is founded in Salerno, Italy, and women are accepted there as students. The school is the first school of its kind that is not affiliated with the Catholic church.
1100	Italian gynecologist Trotula of Salerno writes *Diseases of Women*. It remains an important medical textbook for several centuries.
1348	The Black Death, a plague transmitted by fleas that live on rats, spreads throughout Europe, killing people by the thousands.
1492	The Explorer Christopher Columbus lands on San Salvador, an island in the Bahamas. He claims this New World in the name of the Spanish King Ferdinand.
1601	Frenchwoman Louyse Bourgeois becomes one of the first graduates of the Hôtel-Dieu, a renowned midwifery school in Paris.
1650	A deadly typhus epidemic spreads through Britain.
1671	In England Jane Sharp publishes her influential instructional manual, *The Midwives' Book; or The Whole Art of Midwifery Discovered*.
1699	German entomologist and scientific artist Maria Sibylla Merian sails to Suriname in South America to study and paint the insects there.

Maria Sibylla Merian's illustration of the **Thysania agrippina** *moth*

1709 — The Black Death kills more people in Prussia than in any war, totaling 300,000 deaths.

1718 — The British writer Lady Mary Wortley Montagu publishes her report "Inoculation Against Smallpox."

1760 — The anatomist Anna Manzolini becomes a full professor at the medical school in Bologna, Italy.

1775–1783 — The American Revolution. The Declaration of Independence is signed in July 1776.

1789–1799 — Revolution in France

1798 — Edward Jenner, an English physician, initiates the use of vaccination to fight smallpox. His work is based on the same theory that Lady Montagu discovered and used.

1814 — Renowned French midwife Marie Boivin is given the Order of Merit by King Frederick William II of Prussia.

1819 — German obstetrician Charlotte von Siebold helps to deliver the future Queen Victoria of England.

1835 — Harriot Kezia Hunt and her sister begin providing health care to women and children that is based upon proper diet, hygiene, and regular exercise.

1848 — The first women's rights convention is held in Seneca Falls, New York.

1858 — The first female physician in America, Dr. Elizabeth Blackwell, travels to England. While there, she becomes the first officially recognized female doctor in Great Britain and also inspires Englishwoman Elizabeth Garrett Anderson to study medicine.

1861–1865 — The Civil War in America. Dr. Mary Walker serves as a surgeon for the Union army.

1865 — Dr. James Barry dies in London and is discovered to be a woman named Miranda Stuart. Barry had practiced medicine as a man since she was 18.

1866 — Lucy Taylor is the first American woman to receive a degree in dentistry.

1874 — The Scottish medical student Sophia Jex-Blake and Dr. Elizabeth Blackwell found the London School of Medicine for Women.

1876 — American Dr. Mary Jacobi publishes *Questions of Rest for Women During Menstruation*, in which she contradicts the common notion that women should not participate in everyday activities while they are menstruating.

1877 — British entomologist Eleanor Ormerod publishes the first *Annual Report of Injurious Insects*. The free reports are popular with farmers, who consult them to find out simple and effective ways to deal with harmful pests.

1880 — Physician Emily Jennings Stowe, who was forced to go to the United

Dr. Emily Stowe

States to obtain her medical degree, receives a license to practice in her home country. She is Canada's first woman doctor.

1881 The American Association of the Red Cross is founded by nurse and activist Clara Barton.

1883 Aspiring medical student Anandibai Joshee gives a speech in Calcutta, India, in response to critics who say a Hindu woman should not become a doctor.

1893 M. Carey Thomas, the founder of Bryn Mawr College, and Mary Garrett, a wealthy philanthropist, contribute money to found a medical school at Johns Hopkins University. The catch? The school will have to admit women.

The Botanical Society of America is established. The only woman among the 25 founding members is the moss expert Elizabeth Knight Britton.

1894 American physician Anna Wessels Williams isolates a strain of diphtheria toxin from which she develops an antitoxin that will drastically reduce diphtheria cases.

1895 London-born Lilian Murray Lindsay graduates from the Edinburgh Dental Hospital, becoming the first British woman dentist.

1902 Dr. Ida Henrietta Hyde becomes the first woman member of the American Physiological Association.

1914–1918 World War I. Scottish surgeon Elsie Inglis mobilizes a group of women doctors to aid in the war effort. The volunteers are rejected by the British military, but the French and Belgians gratefully accept their aid.

1915 The American Medical Women's Association is formed by physician Bertha Van Hoosen.

Dr. Bertha Van Hoosen

1918 An epidemic of Spanish influenza sweeps through Asia, Europe, and North America, killing millions.

1919 Dr. Alice Hamilton, a pioneer in the study of hygiene, is named Harvard University's first woman professor.

1920 The 19th Amendment to the United States Constitution grants women the vote. It goes into effect August 26th.

1925 American Dr. Florence Sabin is the first woman elected to the National Academy of Sciences.

1928 Alexander Fleming, the Scottish bacteriologist and future husband of Dr. Amalia Fleming, observes that a kind of mold, *Penicillium notatum*, kills many common bacteria. By using these findings, scientists go on to develop antibiotics that control a number of previously fatal diseases.

1939–1945 World War II. Among the many scientists who are forced to flee

Germany are Tilly Edinger, Frieda Fromm-Reichmann, and Anna Freud.

1945–1954 The Indochinese War. French army physician and helicopter pilot Valerie André acquits herself with honor.

1946 *Sister Kenny*, a Hollywood film starring Rosalind Russell, opens. It honors Australian Elizabeth Kenny, who became a popular heroine for her therapeutic treatment for polio.

1947 Czech-born Gerty Cori and her husband, Carl, biochemical researchers, win the Nobel Prize for their work on the metabolic process.

1949 In China, the Communist party takes over the government. At this time Dr. Lin Ch'iao Chih is a beloved public figure for her work to promote public health.

Barbara McClintock

1951 American geneticist—and future Nobel Prizewinner—Barbara McClintock reveals her innovative theories at a symposium in Cold Springs Harbor, New York.

1952 Dr. Virginia Apgar, an American physician, introduces the "Apgar Score," a system for evaluating

infants immediately after birth to determine potential health problems.

1955 Psychologist Joyce Brothers appears on the television show "The $64,000 Question." Not only does she win the prize, she launches her career as a media personality.

Dr. Jonas Salk introduces a polio vaccine that will practically eliminate the disease.

1959 British paleontologists Mary and Louis Leakey uncover the fossilized molar of a humanlike mammal, *Zinjanthropus*. The tooth is believed to be 1.75 million years old.

1961 American Dr. Hattie Alexander finds a cure for bacterial meningitis.

1962 Dr. Helen Taussig of the U.S. Food and Drug Administration investigates reports that a new sleeping pill, thalidomide, is harmful to unborn infants. The drug is not approved for use in America.

1964–1975 War in Vietnam

1969 Swiss-born psychiatrist Elisabeth Kübler-Ross publishes *On Death and Dying*, encouraging counseling and compassionate treatment for the terminally ill.

1970s Mammography use increases as new and more effective techniques for detecting breast cancer become available. The X rays used are not only less harmful, but they also produce better images.

1975 Anthropologist Margaret Mead becomes one of the first women members of the United States Academy of Sciences.

1977 — Rosalyn Yalow, Roger Guillemin, and Andrew Schally share the Nobel Prize for physiology or medicine for their work in radioimmunoassay.

Wangari Maathai, a Kenyan biologist and environmentalist, founds the Green Belt Movement, training women to plant trees to replace the country's vanishing forests.

1981 — AIDS begins to receive recognition as a serious health problem.

1985 — American pharmacologist Gertrude Elion shares the Nobel Prize in physiology or medicine with George Hitchings and James Black.

American Dian Fossey, who has been living in Africa to study gorillas, is murdered at her camp, probably by someone who resents her campaign to save the primates from poachers.

1986 — Italian-born Dr. Rita Levi-Montalcini and Dr. Stanley Cohen win the Nobel Prize in physiology or medicine for their research on the chemical Nerve Growth Factor.

Biruté Galdikas with an orangutan

1987 — Canadian primatologist Biruté Galdikas, who has been studying orangutans on the island of Borneo, establishes Orangutan Foundation International to help protect the endangered animals.

1989 — The Cold War ends. In Germany, the Berlin Wall is torn down, and the country is reunited.

1990 — President George Bush appoints Dr. Antonia Novello as the surgeon general of the United States. The first woman and the first Hispanic person to fill the post, she serves until early 1993.

1992 — A good year for women astronauts. In January Dr. Roberta Bondar becomes Canada's first woman in space aboard the shuttle *Discovery*. In September, on board the *Endeavour*, Dr. Mae Jemison becomes the first African American woman in space.

1993 — Biologist Margie Profet receives a MacArthur Foundation "genius grant" that allows her to study any topic she chooses. She begins to research birth defects and pregnancy.

1995 — German Christiane Nüsslein-Volhard is a winner of the Nobel Prize for medicine for her work with Eric Wieschaus on genetic mapping.

1996 — Eighty-nine-year-old American environmentalist Ruth Patrick receives the National Medal of Science from President Bill Clinton.

1997 — South African physician and activist Mamphela Ramphele publishes her memoir, entitled *Across Boundaries: The Journey of a South African Woman Leader*.

1999 — Marine biologist and environmentalist Sylvia Earle's book *Dive: My Adventures Undersea* appears.

GLOSSARY

AIDS: Acquired immunodeficiency syndrome, a disease (transmitted by contact with infected blood or body fluids) that destroys the human immune system. Victims are then vulnerable to other illnesses, one of which usually causes death.

Anatomy: the study of the physical structure of plants or animals.

Anesthetics: any of several drugs that temporarily induce the partial or total loss of sensory awareness to pain.

Anthropology: the study of human customs, societies, and their origins.

Antibiotic: any of several drugs used to treat or to cure infectious diseases by destroying or inhibiting the development of bacteria and other disease-causing microorganisms.

Archaeology: the study of vanished cultures through the excavation and examination of their cities and their artifacts.

Autopsy: the dissection and examination of a body to determine the cause of death.

Bacteria (singular form, bacterium): microscopic organisms, each of which consists of only a single cell. Some kinds of bacteria cause diseases, while others are beneficial.

Biochemistry: the branch of chemistry that focuses on the chemical compounds and processes that occur in organisms.

Biofeedback: a technique in which the subject learns to exercise conscious control over physiological processes (such as blood pressure, heart rate, or brain waves) that normally function involuntarily. The goal is to counteract the harmful effects of the body's unconscious reactions to stress.

Botany: the study of plants.

Cadaver: a corpse, usually human, that has been preserved for dissection and study.

Cardiology: the study of the function of the heart and related diseases.

Chemotherapy: the treatment of disease by administering drugs. Chemotherapy is most often associated with the treatment of cancer.

Chromosome: an elongated, microscopic part of the cell that contains hereditary information.

Conchology: the study of shells and the mollusks that inhabit them. Mollusks are a group of soft-bodied creatures that do not have skeletons but usually have shells.

Congenital: existing at the time of birth.

Dispensary: a place where medical care is available. In general, a dispensary provides straightforward treatment, such as first aid or medical supplies.

Ecology: the study of the relationships that exist between organisms and the environments they inhabit.

Ecosystem: a community of living things—plants, animals, and bacteria—whose interrelated life cycles and functions form an environmental unit. Each organism's survival, through a complex series of events, depends on the others.

Embryology: the study of the embryo, the earliest stage of animal development.

Entomology: the study of insects.

Epidemic: literally, something that spreads "among the people." The word is most often used in terms of serious contagious diseases that infect large numbers of people very quickly.

Ethnomusicology: the study of music in the context of its native culture.

Genetics: the branch of biology that deals with the study of hereditary traits and the variations of inherited characteristics.

Gynecology: the study of the female reproductive system and treatment of its related diseases.

Homeopathy: the treatment of disease by administering small doses of substances that would cause symptoms of the disease in healthy people.

Ichthyology: the study of fish.

Inoculate: to administer a serum or vaccination in order to build immunity to a disease.

IQ: or "intelligence quotient." A number intended to indicate relative intelligence. It is calculated by administering tests designed to determine the subject's "mental" age, dividing that number by actual age, then multiplying it by 100.

Membranes: thin layers of tissue in plants and animals that act as barriers to divide and line organs.

Metabolism: the chemical processes in living organisms by which energy and growth are produced.

Midwife: a woman whose profession is to assist pregnant women during childbirth.

Neurobiology: the biological study of the nervous system, encompassing its anatomy, physiology, and pathology.

Neurology: the branch of medicine dealing with the study of the nervous system and the treatment of its diseases.

Neuropathology: the study of the origin and causes of diseases of the nervous system.

Neurosis: a type of psychological disorder that is characterized by such emotions as anxiety, fear, obsession, or depression.

Obstetrics: the branch of medical science that is focused on the care of women throughout pregnancy and childbirth.

Oncology: the study of tumors and their treatment.

Ornithology: the study of birds.

Paleontology: the study of prehistoric life.

Pasteurization: a process developed by the French bacteriologist Louis Pasteur, in which substances are partially sterilized by heating them until harmful organisms are destroyed.

Pathology: the study of the origins, causes, and characteristics of disease.

Phrenology: a now obsolete science based on the idea that the shape of the skull indicates truths about a person's character and intelligence.

Physiology: the study of the vital functions and processes of living organisms.

Psychiatry: the branch of medicine that focuses on emotional or mental health.

Psychoanalysis: a therapeutic method that employs discussion to treat mental disorders.

Psychology: the branch of the social sciences that focuses on human and animal behavior.

Schizophrenia: a mental disease marked by delusions and the separation of thoughts from emotions.

Specimen: a sample obtained for scientific study, or to provide an example of other objects of its kind.

Taxonomy: the science of classifying things. Most often the word is used in relation to the biological sciences to describe the system of grouping plants and animals into categories based on characteristics that they have in common.

Thanatology: the study of the process of dying and of psychological ways to cope with it.

Toxicology: the study of poisons, their effects on the body, and how to counteract them.

Virus: an extremely small—submicroscopic—organism that can only reproduce in living cells and often causes disease.

Zoology: the study of animals.

INDEX

Numbers in boldface type indicate main entries.

CREDITS

Quotes

12 Bailey, Florence A. Merriam. *Birds Through an Opera Glass*. Boston: Houghton, Mifflin and Company, 1893. **18** Cheesman, Evelyn. *Things Worth While*. London: Hutchinson & Co., 1957. **25** Earle, Sylvia Alice. *Sea Change: A Message of the Oceans*. New York: G. P. Putnam's Sons, 1995. Used by permission. **33** Galdikas, Biruté. *Reflections of Eden: My Years with the Orangutans of Borneo*. Boston: Little, Brown and Company, 1995. Used by permission. **37** Horney, Karen. *Final Lectures*. New York: W. W. Norton & Company, 1987. Used by permission. **41** Jex-Blake, Sophia. *Medical Woman: A Thesis and a History*. Edinburgh: Oliphant, Anderson, & Ferrier, 1886. **43** Kenyon, Kathleen. *Beginning Archaeology*. London: Phoenix House Limited, 1961. **59** Rothschild, Miriam Louisa. *Fleas, Flukes & Cuckoos: A Study of Bird Parasites*. New York: Philosophical Library, 1952. Used by permission. **65** Van Hoosen, Bertha. *Petticoat Surgeon*. Chicago: Pellegrini & Cudahy, 1947.

Photographs

Abbreviations

COR Corbis
HG Hulton Getty
LOC Library of Congress
MCP Archives and Special Collections on Women in Medicine, MCP Hahnemann University,
SSC The Sophia Smith Collection, Smith College

8 Aldrich-Blake, Louisa, LOC. **9** Andersen, Dorothy, LOC. **10** André, Valerie, LOC. **11** Apgar, Virginia, LOC. **12 (and title page)** Baker, Sara, LOC; **13** Benedict, Ruth, LOC. **14 (and 6)** Bondar, Roberta, NASA. **16** Britton, Elizabeth, The LuEsther T. Mertz Library of the New York Botanical Garden, Bronx, NY; Brothers, Joyce, LOC. **17 (and cover)** Carson, Rachel, LOC. **19** Chinn, May, MCP; Clapp, Cornelia Maria, The Mount Holyoke Archives and Special Collections. **21 (and cover)** Cori, Gerty, LOC. **22** Dalle Donne, Maria, LOC; Densmore, Frances, LOC. **24** Downs, Cornelia, LOC. **25** Eckstorm, Fannie, Bangor Public Library. **26** Edinger, Tilly, COR. **27 (and 6)** Elders, Jocelyn, University of Arkansas School for the Medical Sciences. **28** Evans, Alice, LOC. **29** Fleming, Amalia, COR/Hulton-Deutsch Collection. **30** Fletcher, Alice, National Anthropological Archives, National Museum of Natural History, Smithsonian Institution. **31** Fossey, Dian, COR. **32 (and title page)** Freud, Anna, LOC. **34** Gimbutas, Marija. Photo credit: M. Djordjevic, Belgrade: courtesy of Bata Galovic. **35** Goodall, Jane, LOC. **36 (and 7)** Hamilton, Alice, LOC. **37** Hollingworth, Leta. From *Leta Stetter Hollingworth: A Biography*. University of Nebraska Press. **39** Hurd-Mead, Kate, MCP; Hyman, Libbie, LOC. **40** Jacobi, Mary Putnam from *Dictionary of American Portraits*. New York: Dover Publications, 1967. **41 (and cover)** Jemison, Mae, NASA. **42** Jordan, Sara, LOC. **43** Kenny, Elizabeth, HG. **44** King, Helen, The Wistar Institute. **45** Kübler-Ross, Elisabeth, COR/Jack Moebes. **46** Leakey, Mary, COR/Bettmann. **47** Lozier, Clemence, LOC. **48** Maathai, Wangari, COR/Adrian Arbib. **49 (and title page)** Mead, Margaret, Courtesy of the National Archives, photo number: 208-PU-134K-6. **50** Mendenhall, Dorothy, SSC. **52 (and 7)** Montagu, Mary, HG; Nayar, Shushila, LOC. **54** Panajiotatou, Angeliki, MCP. **55** Parsons, Elsie, COR. **56** Picotte, Susan La Flesche, MCP. **57** Powdermaker, Hortense, LOC. **58** Rathbun, Mary Jane, LOC. **59** Sabin, Florence, LOC. **60** Shabanova, Anna, MCP. **61** Slye, Maud, LOC. **62** Stuart, Miranda, HG. **63** Taussig, Helen, LOC. **64** Thompson, Mary, MCP. **66** Walker, Mary, LOC. **67** Webb, Beatrice, HG; Westheimer, Ruth, COR/Mitchell Gerber. **69 (and title page)** Wright, Jane, LOC. **70** Yalow, Rosalyn, LOC. **71** "A Surinam Portfolio" by Maria Merian. From *Natural History Magazine*, December 1962. © *Natural History Magazine*, SSC. **72** Stowe, Emily, LOC. **73** Van Hoosen, Bertha, MCP. **75** McClintock, Barbara, HG. **75 (and cover)** Galdikas, Biruté, The Orangutan Foundation International.